marmalade

ali lanzetta

SPUYTEN DUYVIL
New York City

Reading ali lanzetta is like running wild all summer with someone you share a secret language with. Her writing is playful, soulful, profuse, and altogether alive. It's the work of someone who's made up her mind that you two are going to be great friends.

Mike DeCapite, author of *Jacket Weather*

This book is pure magic with its perfect storm of wit, heartbreak, joy and unrelenting hope. I want to invoke the language from within but I don't possess the magic to capture the complexities and brilliance of ali lanzetta's *marmalade* in a single statement. You'll just have to read this for yourself and know that you will be forever changed. Can we as readers be kinder having experienced the language and presence of the writer, of another? I say yes. It is here in this time, in this gift of a book.

Truong Tran, author of *book of the other*

In *marmalade*, ali lanzetta's wondrous debut book, each page, each poem shines forthwith a voice as singular and full of light as you'll ever find. Here is a poet who writes with humor, depth, revelation, wonder, and it's a wonder how she does it but she does. In her poem, "escape hatch", we find the lines, "i smartly broke the moment. this, my area of expertise, the shimmering snap." This book is full to the brim of that shimmering snap, and her one-of-a-kind, smart, lyrical voice breaks in, breaks the moment, breaks us out of any malaise or doubt we might feel these days. John Steinbeck once wrote of his desire to "spread each page with shining." This is just what ali lanzetta has done, page after page after page.

Toni Mirosevich, author of *Spell Heaven*

for Olive

I hope the dancers do a good job of it,
they hold our imaginations in their feet.

RICHARD BRAUTIGAN

~ : ~

My imagination is a monastery and I am its monk.

JOHN KEATS

~ : ~

When danger approaches, sing to it.

ARAB PROVERB

~ : ~

contents

marmalade

i'll have what i'm having.
my poem that knows how to be everything without knowing
everything.
for example, a new dance that levitates you.
how to swallow a disco ball and use your breath to spin it.
one word that turns on the light but inside your mouth.
a canary in heaven. actually all of them.
sunshine to match like matching outfits.
a yellow that's daffodil yellow and when everybody sees that
color they think of me.

notes preceding a new rhapsodic broadcast

Figure 1. i think i have a crush on this owl.

weaver of truths that i am, some of the lines between things get fuzzy. but sometimes, if you blur the edges, the middle of the photo comes into a sharper focus—i'm thinking about documenting bridges.

some initial ideas about my potential documentation process:
i'm a library and also the librarian. or,
my imagination is a museum and i am the
curator! or,
i'm hoarding a particular history. collecting bits of dream, boundary, language, memory, shells and twigs and leaves and animals and lightning bugs in jars to illuminate something i don't know i'm looking for. arranging and rearranging, as if a dollhouse, as bookshelf, as if a bric-a-brac garden. "documenting" becomes more malleable a process of discovering and saving. or,

maybe peeking out from under all of my work is really a love letter to the universe. flip that rock over. see?

for the record, as a reckless and amateur philosopher i've surrendered to this, as my general M.O.:

solipsism |sälip-sizəm|
noun
the theory that the self is all that can be known to exist. or,
the belief that all reality is just one's own imagining of reality, and that one's self is the only thing that exists.

ORIGIN late 19th cent.: from Latin *solus* 'alone' + *ipse* 'self' + -ism.

moving right along, here is a list of what i am considering for my documentarian purposes:
1. bridges, boundaries, edges. what happens at those places.
2. my own constantly shifting sense of place in the universe.
3. our abstract relationships to the natural world (see fig. 1).

i've also been considering starting a project about the disappearance of Amelia Earhart, but hesitate to dive in because i am not Amelia Earhart.

the thing about the "lyric" part is that if you have a particularly WIDE associative net, as some folks most certainly do, your documentary about, say, *starfish* seems to become more about bioluminescence than starfish, then more about submarines than bioluminescence, then more about sunken ships than submarines, then more about prehistoric sharks than sunken ships, then more about dreaming about sharks than prehistoric sharks, then more about dreaming about flying than dreaming about sharks, then more about birds or airplanes than about dreaming about flying, then more about space travel than birds or airplanes, then more about the moon in particular than about space travel, and the moon in particular regulates the tides and the tides circle right back around to the starfish.

to summarize: there's an inherent poetry in the process of leaping.

i'm interested in documenting everything that i learn, and how it relates (imaginatively, mnemonically, hunter-like) to me, my Self (the only thing that exists).
i'm going to write a book about that. did i mention i'm learning french? it's going to be called:
l'encyclopédie de ce que je connais or, "the encyclopedia of what i know"

here i go!

lyrical
adjective
1 expressive, emotional, deeply felt, personal, subjective, passionate, lyric.
2 enthusiastic, rhapsodic, effusive, rapturous, ecstatic, euphoric, carried away.
antonym: unenthusiastic. *(pas que je connais!)*

documentary | ˌdäkyə'mentərē |

adjective

1 recorded, documented, registered, written, chronicled, archived, on record, on paper, in writing.

2 factual, nonfictional.

noun

factual program, factual film; program, film, broadcast

A FINAL CONFESSION (shh):

i have long suspected that whether i necessarily want to or not, i seem to be ever-tangled in the mischievous business of looking, usually, to get carried away.

i woke up smelling like a horse—i'd been dreaming of jumping over the moon, over it and over and over again.

"i smell like a horse," i said. "do you think i smell like a horse?"
he shrugged. "it doesn't matter what you smell like," he said, "because you are a horse."
the field was rimmed with buttercups. they made a buttery ruffle around it, melting brightly in the hot, high july light. fireflies were asleep in the tall grass, their bellies blinking, warm and unseen.

i munched a sprig of clover and shook a fly away, thinking hard.

"if i'm a horse," i said finally, "what are you?"
he looked at me like a carrot.
"i'm a trail through the woods," he said.

when one hoof scraped it, a little clink of sunlit moon twinkled off. *one more time*, i thought, *if i jump just one more time.*

paris, a promise, sticking your fingers in your ears and singing

promise | ˈpräməs |

n. an assurance that something will happen

n. the quality of potential excellence

PHRASES

promise (someone) *the earth* (or moon)

make extravagant promises to someone that are unlikely to be fulfilled

promises, promises

used to indicate that the speaker is skeptical about someone's stated intention to do something.

—

i'm going all out, moon-crash, yard-sale. i can be sweeter than i promised, i promise, but i promise with my fingers crossed.

i was trying to write a poem about a cosmic bake-sale (neptunian wind, star cakes, etc.) but my violet imagination won't let me up out of the sand, where i've stuck my head in a hole and now have a lot of dirt up my nose. i mean ears, eyes, i mean i was trying to emerge from the muck like a star seed, primordial cat's tooth, a phoenix. trying.

hiding in the forest is difficult if you live in the city. the urban foresters are a contradiction in terms. it's unfortunate. i've heard that paris has the most trees of any city in the world but the oldest tree in paris is dead. i'd like to visit, if only to sit on a bench in *Le Bois de Boulogne*, which doesn't translate (wooded port?) and watch a cloud pass over the december sun, throwing a long shadow across the frosted grasses, where a green-gray pond reflects back a black statue of kissing once the shadow passes.

in short: i am trying to write a poem that is like learning french and moving to paris, where i want it to be winter. maybe this is that poem, or maybe it isn't. but i don't want you to come.

i want to go by myself which poses a (not unpoetic) problem, but i have a lot of things to talk to all those old trees about. with all the poems, la dee da, i'm trying to nurture my bad habit of talking to everything except people. the difference between the way a person listens and a tree or a dog or a streetlamp listens is that people listen with their mouths full. trees listen with their quiet ache of growing and of being an only, of a stretch in all directions toward something and being able to reach but not relocate. and when you ask them a question they reply by turning bright yellow, and it takes a long time, a steadfast hugging of something underground, all that stoic reach and rustle. i don't think i'm kidding and i didn't dream it, or if i did, i dreamt it because it happened.

where the green grass falls into the water, there's a stone curb. good for pushing a foot over, testing the temperature. you could drown in an inch of water on a bad day but this is going to be a good day, because the trees have turned yellow, and you're in paris, and the sky has turned whitish-yellow, and you're wearing a scarf and mittens and it's almost winter. the sound dies down, the flowers bend in a sleepy droop and collapse in a last laughter, completely exhausted. "encore!' you shout, "bravo, *dames fu-tées! c'est magnifique!*" but you know from their scented smiles, bent to the ground, that there won't be a second act. you breathe into your wooly hands and rub them together in a kind of mit-ten-song to resolve the moment, or maybe to resolve all of them.

"the word for language," you either read or decide, "is the same as the word for tongue." meaning that's where it lives. or in that case, couldn't it be the same as the word for looking, or longing, or winter, or bewilder? be-wilder. you step quietly back from de-ciding into wonder, re-crossing the line like legs. language is a quiet thing, or should be. don't come to paris. i want to travel the world alone, sipping a breeze or a teacup on park benches with very tiny birds balanced on very long branches, all of us sticking our fingers in our ears and singing, wearing little honey-colored shoes. there's so much to listen for, no time for small-talk. large-talk throws pictures against the seeds and stars, its narrative al-ways populated with heroes and ghosts, against the disappear-ing act (maybe you can see them or maybe you can't!) like how the sun rises every morning to wipe your dreams away like the breath-mist-words on the tree-sized window where i drew mine between us. i am trying to promise, i promise! promises, prom-ises.

—

bewilder
ORIGIN
late 17th century: from be-'thoroughly' + obsolete *wilder* 'lead or go astray', of unknown origin.

wanderlust home

a dress made of poems, i thought, a paper-dress for a paper-girl. you're no paper-girl she said. who am i. you're a little blue egg with a bird inside. i'm a bird. you're that blurry star the sun makes for the camera. i'm a star? you're a camera. you make faces. i am trying to see the big picture through you. you're a road atlas with scribbles all over it. really. yes. you're the pages torn out. someone's imaginary friend. really i said. it goes both ways. well pleased to meet you, i never did figure that out. plunk. lake-water-me looks over grass-stained-me's shoulder. my grass-stains are shaped like knees. knees are shaped like scabs shaped like band-aids. the clouds are shaped like clouds. plunk. the clouds are shaped like broken airplanes.

some people sneak around on the internet looking at porn. girls eating poo from a cup. some guy jerking off into his wife's shoes. stuff like that. i sneak around looking at this new hampshire real estate website. it's called Bean Group. what the hell does that mean. maybe someone named Bean started it. maybe it's like jack and the bean, how he started out all tiny in his crumby hole in the ground then whoosh up he went on his magical bean to the clouds. is that how it goes. so close to the stars you could singe your eyelashes. maybe that's what this group is all about. i don't know who they are but i love them. back yard abuts conservation land, Bean says. easy commute to boston. mature fruit trees. peek-a-boo. sometimes my mom's in on the game. that yellow one is so cute i can't stand it, let's buy dad a castle. sale pending. eleven extra photos. longing fills me like liquid. it's easier to breathe. sitting up in bed glassy-eyed at pictures of wooden kitchens with millions of baskets hanging. captivated by the made-up prospect of owning magic beans. backdrop of bus doors folding and un-folding down the block, plexiglas wings on a clumsy bird. open, close. open, close. cabs shoot by in the night.

my mother always hung baskets from the beams. josh used to hang upside-down on them like a giant sloth. maybe i was suck-ing my thumb or eating grapes maybe i thought i was at the zoo. either way looking up. i was always looking. oh my look, would you look at those big eyes. grown-ups would ask me a question and i would just look at them. look out from behind the corner of my curled fist. little pointer finger snailed around my nose. oh it's okay. she never takes her thumb out of her mouth. josh would talk for me. her name's ali. she's four. she's pleased to meet you.

my name is ali. i'm twenty-eight. i live in san francisco. you've never met me. that's all you really need to know.

the noontime announcer on public radio says later there will be a guy on the show who was eight years old when he watched his mother slit her wrists and write his name in blood on the wall. i think about my mother drinking coffee in the sun leaning against the kitchen counter. balancing the phone on her shoulder. watch-ing my dad knock the icicles down and fill the birdfeeders for the blue jays and purple finches. sun on bare grey branches. maybe the cardinals were my favorite. bright red against white. chickadees are mom's favorite i think. look at the chickadees. look. little birdfeet make arrows all discombobulated in the snow. that's her word. it's chinaberry i tell her. blooming. that's why my block smells so sweet. ack. but it's february. balancing the phone on my shoulder. come visit later for the lilacs she says, and we'll plant you a cantaloupe.

i can't remember what happened to jack. the houses all have something green somewhere around them. they have the sky behind them like toy houses in a sky theater. that clean blue that means north. that means birds who have never seen a sidewalk. for a while when i was in maybe the third grade, i probably wanted to build sceneries for theaters. when i am twenty-eight i want them again and also a messy playwright lover. if i built theater sceneries i would paint them all blue. fee fi fo fum. when you see pictures of jesus, like in your grandmother's florida bedroom on a little wooden plaque near the light switch, his eyes are the color of the sky. do they do that on purpose. my mother grows bright green beans and basil. clean cucumber and mint. puts it in her water and drinks it. my mother believes in birds and doesn't believe in god.

Dear Mom,
I'll take this one. It's even older than our house. Look at the garden. You guys can come over and help me plant it. We can plant

watermelons and cherry tomatoes and eggplant. Jake and Elwood can come over and play with Olive while we're gardening.
I like that it's blue with red trim. How adorable.
I would like to buy and move in to it immediately.
Love,
Premenstrual Syndrome In The City

new hampshire thinks the west coast is hula hoops. a coast of flimsy flower-people. new hampshire drives its truck out onto the middle of the lake and sits with its pole in the snow. steaming black coffee hot from a thermos. slurp. light a cigarette. slurp. sun coming up like a grapefruit. lights another one. little nose-hairs frozen. comparing the sun to various fruits, new hampshire thinks i'm worldly. how 'bowt that cyurious one, new hampshire says. that theya little one from the treefaam up theya by Miles' place, go-on off to be somebody. yup. new hampshire i love you. new hampshire wait for me. new hampshire. wanderlust is over-rated. new hampshire the west coast is bright mango slime is flowers all year and nothing dies you're right. new hampshire plant me a pumpkin. new hampshire sit down with my heart. stuffed the last of my maps in a picnic basket and buried in the garden. roll out your carpet of mudsalt and snow to tug me home.

mom said the last storm brought so much snow, the plow guy had to come with a backhoe. a whole new layer to the earth. you should come in the spring. when the first tulips shoot up through the ice. the grass in hibernation down there. under the world with the worms. under that old foundation, which is like the ground, laid down in 1775. it says so on the chimney. but not everyone signed the Declaration of Independence she said. in the spring. the birds make such a racket. everything's new.

when my first love—leaf—was a kid, his family had no money. he desperately wanted this remote-controlled airplane for christmas. maybe he was seven. his parents couldn't afford it. no way we can't afford that. on christmas morning the three kids sat in the living room by the tinsel tree and opened their presents. tore off the paper and there it was. the airplane. holy crap. the airplane! could hardly contain himself. ran outside little barefoot. los angeles christmas morning it's 68 degrees and mostly clear. some of the smog melted off. got the plane up in the sky. the plane is flying. he's flying it. he's a pilot. he's sailing over the neighborhood. he's flying flying, higher and higher until the plane is just a spec. flying off toward the world. ahh. o.k. turn around now. turn. he doesn't know how to turn. come back, plane. come back. take me with you. turn. it won't turn. he doesn't know how. he wants to go with it, wants it to come back. he doesn't know. so off it goes without him. no. he never sees it again. merry christmas.

when i leave it's summer, the middle. like the part where you're thirteen and have bug bites all over, even on your butt from sitting in shorts in the grass sneaking cigarettes behind the barn watching the sun go down past the pine trees. here's a picture: i have two braids in my hair. i'm sitting at the wheel of my brother's station wagon, both of which are dropping me off in my new state of oregon. i am to cruise down the driveway to the road that goes to another and another for three thousand and fifty-three miles. i am twenty. i'm grinning. yeah i'm doing it and i don't care get me outta here. manifest destiny, man. i have maps. i have sunglasses and coffee. i have my brother who hates both cat stevens and cigarettes so i have to wait until he's asleep in the passenger seat for all that. here's my mom off to the side with the birds. just be careful. who probably have tears in their eyes. bird-tears. put on your seatbelt says my dad. and don't sleep at truckstops. live free or die says new hampshire. be careful. keep your eyes on the road. don't forget new hampshire.

josh had this, his favorite hat. if it's not on his head he put it on the dashboard. it's too hot for hats. somewhere in one of those vowel states, iowa, ohio, illinois, indiana, something, we are in a nasty yelling car-fight and i roll down my window and his hat flies off the dashboard and is sucked into outer space. he is so mad i think he will give himself an aneurysm. i am laughing like crazy because i'm nervous he might kill me and i really need a cigarette and i also know that the next exit is in like five million miles because i saw a sign. i think i won the fight by default. over the next six years he will keep trying to move away from new england and won't. i will live in permanently moveable places, tents and vans and various couches coast-to-coast. for a while i even lived in a cave which is not moveable on some beach on this island but it did fill up with the ocean when it was autumn and the tide comes up. we had to evacuate. what was out came in. our stolen plastic salt and pepper shakers floating. get the guitar.

has anyone seen my other shoe. did you even have another shoe. ali get your shell collection. some people got stung by manowar. they had to pee on the stings because that's the cure for it. and there was a giant sea turtle, i saw him.

my name is ali. i have a van with expired plates from north carolina, whose state motto is "a better place to be". up until 1893 they were the only one of the original thirteen states without a motto. i have an oregon driver's license, which has a hologram of evergreen trees. i graduated from the evergreen state college in washington state. i have one brother who is 13 months older who has a fiancé and a dog and a house in colorado. my best friend is colleen searcy who has pumpkin-colored hair and lives in ohio. i am twenty-eight and my address is 1992 grove street san francisco california 94117. my phone number is 782-9277. the area code is (603) which is new hampshire, which everybody thinks is weird.

fireflies actually don't bite. evidently they are capable of biting, but they choose not to. i just made that up. i don't actually know if they have teeth or not. i kind of doubt it. they have light-emitting organs in their bellies. for christsake. female fireflies glow 1. to attract mates and 2. to lure other bugs in to eat them. maybe at one point new hampshire seriously considered making its state-insect a firefly, but the legislature never put the measure to a vote. i'm not telling you this so you'll go there. i don't actually want you to go there. when i go there i want everything to be exactly how i left it.

maybe

is a snail being sung from its shell, is a little key that must open
something (*is this yours?*) but no one knows what. maybe is a
once upon a time there was a bird, the end. once upon a maybe
is a secret wish left ajar upon a time. maybe is a double rainbow
you didn't see because you were facing the other way, maybe says
look! and vanishes in a shimmer. maybe holds its bright hand
flat like the wing of an airplane above its eyes to guard them
from the glare of choosing, to see, to see further than you, to
consider the glimmer as a maybe. maybe is a mystic bending the
light, is a seed twinkling its way on the wind, maybe is what you
both know and don't know you don't know. maybe over heres
and theres and over theres, is fireflies winking on and off, yes/
no leaning together to whisper, the space around or between or
beyond things. maybe is both a sea of dark wrapped around a
bright bead and a bright bead of light blazing in the darkness.
maybe is waving its flag in the vanishing point, squinting, hum-
ming under its breath, is what's always and almost there (*see? just
there...*) in the wisp.

resolutions

1. write every day
write prompts on a log. here's one, from heart of darkness: you will make a glorious lot of smoke anyhow. ha! even if there's a frog sitting on it, singing. (listen for more frogs singing.)

2. get better job
get the keys to the kingdom. when you get home, remember where you put them. DON'T LOCK THEM IN THE CAR! or when you do lock them in the car and you draw an amateur locksmith on the rear windshield with your purple crayon, and he sneaks up behind you while you're sneaking a cigarette and pops you on the bottom with his coat hanger and says *boo!* really quietly in your ear, be careful how you startle so your mom doesn't see.

3. get more sleep
paint things 'in the nude'. all the things! all the time.

4. read more
use the word *akimbo* more. some phrases you could try: *she stood with arms* akimbo, *frowning at the year ahead.* wait! here's a better one: *she stood, her heart akimbo, cursed once, folded it twice under her breath, shifted her weight to her head, and stepped off the edge of herself into the dazzling sweep of days sparking before her like... like...*

5. stop procrastinating
not like stars, not like raindrops. wait—maybe *exactly* like rain-drops?! wait a minute—

6. be on time
listen to yourself as if playing the violin. travel beyond the rim and ruffle of the moment, the hour, of your prickly habits, of believing only what you see. if someone says *you have to see it to believe it*, but you can't see it, believe it anyway.

7. travel more
forget to transform all circumstances into planks on the path of enlightenment. if anyone questions this (nobody will), pre-tend to remember. quote don quixote ("make hay while the sun shines!") or dorothy parker ("clutch it and it may dart away!"). quote yourself, quote yourself more. *if you're a good rider,* yourself can say, *your mind can wander and you won't fall off the horse.*

8. lose 7 lbs.
sip new pennies flicker-winking in a fishpond of wishes you've nipped from stars. or raindrops. (OR RAINDROPS!!!)

9. put yourself "out there"
bring forth what is within you so that it can save and not destroy you, bend gently at your wit's end like a kite bent over a lap of wind, anchored by the slender miscalculating lengths of your jalopy heart, which will be crossing and uncrossing its fingers.

10. whatever you want, go for it!

people say if you want God to grant your wishes, you have to believe in Him, which is the same thing they say about Santa. i wonder about the logic in this. people believe they have swirling wheels of color dotted up their spines, too (like buttons on a snowperson, i guess) and that the wheels can be out of whack (from gunning it instead of slowing down for too many speed bumps), and that each wheel has a name (sharon, pierre, etc.). people believe all sorts of things and a lot of it doesn't add up. spilled salt is bad luck, but sidewalk pennies are good. bird poop, bunny feet: good, good (but not if it's the right foot and not if it's attached to the bunny, in either case neutral). if you eat asymmetrical foods (strawberries with noses, for example) you'll have an ugly baby—bad. and don't walk backwards: it shows The Devil where you're going. you can get any wish from a broken wishbone, any at all, but you just have to be sure and it can't be your own.

vanishing point

we finish our dreams, slippery, push each one into each other's mouths like warm berries. *there are only two stories*, he says. a small, wet knot holds him together. *someone new shows up, or someone goes on a journey.* it's the same thing, i think. our blue-blood hearts, the horizon berry-colored. he squeezes it, and a dream drops out. *there's only one story*, he says, and looks right at me, which is like looking away. *someone loses something.*

dear / dear

1.

use your neurons efficiently. i've been saying it for years. dad is like a crazy person. he gets this health report. i like to do one thing at a time. your uncle says hello and goodbye. just when things are looking great, a mess shows up. this ink will not dry on this paper. i need to sit with a cup of tea in the sunroom, get out my dictionary, if it weren't for that floppy dog i never would have known. let me know when you get these socks.

your avocado pit is in its paper bag in the cupboard.

the leaves are starting to fall today. i'm not ready for winter yet. too many windows. too many flowers to put in the ground. "dance your way to december," your grandma always said, it's always about dancing. i could have stayed in the museum longer, rockefeller center, empire state building, the staten island ferry. sometimes i miss the old brownstones, but the air is crisp, and apples are delicious. i saw a huge deer in the back field yesterday. right out at our tree line by the Miles' side. the goldfinches are everywhere, are such a bright yellow.

here is a blanket with a picture of a house on it. i couldn't resist.

2.

somewhere faraway, a dog drinks out of a birdbath with the blue jays. mosquitoes. the fat round tops of apple trees. do you still haul your wounded apples to the woods for the deer? here's the list i compiled for your recipe:

1. a rainy-day toad in the grass who pees on you when you pick him up.

2. a finger pointing like an arrow. smudgeprint. the postman's "ACK!" a return-to-sender stamp.

3. a dog drinking out of a birdbath.

is this how history perpetuates itself? i put wheat germ or black pepper. i put cinnamon, lemon, "teabags for bruises!", i put it on everything. everything you said. i am a girl with a teacup on my head. my poison oak and love handles healing. the problem of bittersweet and jetty, glittery snowdrifts, the kitchen window. here, it's a problem of can't see the lunar eclipse through the streetlights, or snazzy hairdo dogs eating garbage in the park. here, where bus drivers keep running everyone over. i want to play in the blueberries instead, or storm an abandoned castle. want to? i bet good birds live there. and gnomes, for dad, with pointy hats.

it's just that those double-consonant words are tricky and always trip me up, and the whole thing is like that. which thing goes where?

the apples, the trees. the mistakes that planes make, pretending to be the moon. my musical feminist hero having tendonitis and a baby, i don't know what the world is coming to.

i'm starting to sound like you.

here is a picture of me, cut out of the picture. i took it by mistake.

how to (write a story)

start at age la dee da and don't stop! trade new york and paris for spinning yourself beautifully like a quartet, starting everywhere. be linked and prolific, an accident of karma, a single street of lustrous muscle, spitting distance from peacocks and right next to a church. numbers may be useful: 100, for instance. diems to carpe, men to seduce, all-time slices of cake captured, corsets to unlace. if you get tied up in a dungeon, by way of apology, yawn and say, "i'm actually quite shy in my life as a person," and when they say it can't be, be bashful but fluent and follow the bunny back out of the trap. set traps for yourself to be funneled into books, or blurts, or ice cream cones or congratulations. let luminosity lean out from your structure, the lyrical glimpse, the not-getting-bogged, the reverse-weeping which means laughing. have plenty of reasons to give up, then don't. nod to the flock of stories that follow you. the power of the first person is in the gap between things. rewrite the furniture in light of the flowers! write a story called *the future of my beautiful room* then inhabit it. dish up the dirt when it makes an appearance at the dinner party. put everyone's cherry on top of everyone else's. start and don't stop and let your sense of spinning embody you beyond it.

fairy tale

when i was in love with that married man (fern), everything was an apple and every apple was a sad one, and he had obsidian doe eyes and was cumin colored, but moved like a bird and played the world like a magic piano. the last person i slept with before i met my mr. timeshifter Zen fixer listener quietlight Forever-Person (greg) was a bipolar antiques dealer (ethan) who lived in a little room behind his antique shop in the cobblestone alleyway of a very old port town on the tiny colonial coast of new hampshire— after getting kicked out of an old moneyed new england college for staging a make-believe bomb scare during a manic episode.

exactly none of these men would have understood each other whatsoever.

fern kissed me in feathery dreams, and tasted of midnight and wandering and secrets and apricots. ethan kissed me under the faded ruffle of a streetlit victorian umbrella on a balmy midsummer's eve where i kicked up one heel like a projector-crackled silent movie starlet. greg looks at me squarely before kissing me, like he did in the doorway this morning, the smiling glint in his eyes tinkling, pearl-like, in the glowing space between our faces, only ever right now.

"i'm analog," i like to say. "and you're digital."
"i'm both," he says, happily, fixing my something broken electric.

some words that start with my name: alias, alibi, alien, alight, align, alike, alive, and my current favorite, aliform, adjective, meaning "wing-shaped".

i am trying to
- file the lint of my memory in a grand palm-less pocket, but the pocket has a hole.
- extend an unflinching blush, fragrant simmer, tip the brim of my bonnet, be more petal thicket, abracadabra.
- live in a state of care, thanksgiving, celebrate, adorate. some times the snow is falling and the windows are white and bright and i am alone in a snowglobe with new or made-up words for the world and nobody is kissing me and nothing is now and it is enough.

the thanks-for-the-lift list

2   is there a word for this? i've rummaged through all my books. i've unfolded the paper scraps from all my drawers and cupboards. i've scooped things out from under my bed looking for a word, and instead i found all these other things with names. a flying trapeze artist, a plastic giraffe heart, an X-rayed ribcage with a cricket inside. a wound-up scroll of botanical blueprints for invented fruit. i keep a box of clouds under the mattress. but is there a name for this? this giving words like gifts to hold in our mouths, rolling them around like marbles. warming them, wetting them, to push them through the walls.

3   the possibilities of rainy day imagination: a flea shot out of a cannon. a top-hat full of wild strawberries! this bad sense of direction but this drawing maps on our hands. this wearing a bell for a compass, for the figuring-out of round places. the potential of the made-up places we come from: my first home the burrow of a snowy owl in a maple tree. sticky. think about this: the inherent possibilities of sensual sciences. of collaboration. of collected rainwater, to sift, to skim, to rinse in. to wallpaper this new collapsible space between bodies.

4   the discovery of a blackberry patch under my bed. how does all this stuff get under there?! i was so hungry and paling until now. my sheets and fingers are stained purple and speckled with seeds. i am loading the leftover apples into the wheel-

barrow and wheeling them into the woods for the animals. with all these berries, i may never have to eat an apple again!

5 unlock your chest and let me in. i want to look around. i wouldn't trust a man who didn't kiss his violin, however secretly. let's keep putting your foot in your mouth. it's okay. i'm a bucket of turtle bones and clover. i fall over like autumn. i surrender, splatter the blocks. i am plagued by telepathic wanderlust. among other things. shah. it's a secret. everything you've ever heard about my mouth is true. sit still and i'll show you.

7 what should i be? i'll be everything. whatever weird thing is balanced between the punctuated letters of this new bodily alphabet. i'll be the momentum, the seduction of ellipses. a sideways look with a bit lip. or i'll be the confession, the sultry suggestion of parentheses. the dot dot dots tapped on the window. sun falling away like a string of pearls from the long slender neck of the sky. connected dots with fingertips make pictures to climb in through. look::

9 the lift of forget, of these little gifts that can recreate the scape. don't ask me to say what i lost—in this lost place i had to find, i'm not sure-- glass bowls filled with apple seeds, sharp salty sea-fog, knotted bits of string, hand-drawn memories of snakes—i found these blank bits of paper. to crumple. to dump up into the dark sky like snow. to make a paper-bit snow angel in the street. maybe better not to spell myself in

mouse-bones in a pothole puddle. better maybe: to show you how to draw my name on your lips with my finger. it's true, what you said, if only the world would be full of people kissing in doorways.

static,

static, a cupboard in the heart clicked open. inside, a large spool of thread. radio-colored. slender filament. i disconnect everything that will disconnect, untangling, electric. i hold us one by one to the light, or you can. dear victor, but it's all connected.

a spout, a singing of a bridge and its slatted imagination, i guess we're both on it and inside it, attempting to take leave and take cover which are sometimes one and the same. the leaves on the breeze that wheel up like birds, whirling, when they snap/plunge their scarlet hearts, as i think and hope we will.

my hello waits for yours, carried across the lawn like a secret seed. i've spent the whole day trying to remember the word for the moon, the house, the default setting. there are so many words for falling. slope, slant, grace, surrender, so i can always fall back on the poem. or i'll run up ahead, and you fall behind.

we fall in love, we fall for the trick, the old teacup, singing, fell apart in my hands, as i knew it would. hook, line, and sinker, the roof falls in, or the soldiers do, songlike, but let's not fall in over something so silky, so silly, so rose-glasses, so empty fistful falling asleep in an image's arms. i trip over my own words and fall out. my party dress inflates like a parachute, falling furniture down the hollow underground trunk of the tree we're growing all these poems on. (look up!)

remember in wonderland, how she falls down the rabbit hole in a frantic tumble, as in being chased or chasing or both, as in escape hatch, hinged panel, day/dream, then her wonder catches the air and she floats the rest?

the truth is that the tunnel is a sanctuary, the falling its enchant-ed harbor. poems back and forth are like soft hooks, slant, nearly hands—like holding hands in mittens. my imaginary mailbox a revolving bookcase, kaleidoscopic. false-fixed but, if you look at it right, propped and glittering along the crack. there.

i'm hanging a wordy picture of me on the wall of an unfamiliar ladder-holding heart, using my heart like a ladder so tall you can't see the top, heart like a room with so many doors, or things on high shelves, or things to fall off of. or diorama heart with a paper moon and make-believe trees that actually grow. (see?) teeming topiary heart, tendrils trimmed in a bridge heart to heart. heart jangling in its frame like a fussy window. heart that clunks shut like the hatch to the attic, heart that swings wide like a barn door. heart full of horses, flying across the sun-and-buttercup hills of the heart. heart sweeping the floor. heart with its arms up. fog-horn heart. fire trap heart. heart at the party, sitting on its hands. heart with the price of a poem: to fall in love with everything, all of it. somebody somewhere must understand it like this.

just like this.

it's my birthday. when i wake up i can't remember my dream. i get out of bed and find a note i left myself last night, pink sharpie scrap paper, leaning on the ledge under the bathroom mirror. *happy birthday! i love you.* my hair is a mess. L leaves a message later in the morning - *happy birthday. i love you!* he has a way of being everywhere. i spend some of the morning wondering if R will call, and knowing that he won't. he reminds me of home. i decide to go out. in the botanical garden, i watch a fat man feed peanuts to a fat squirrel. two ladies stand up the path a little, looking alarmed. he looks up and his face is sad and crooked, like a painting with a snag in it. i walk up 9th ave. looking for an ice cream parlor i went to with S once, and can't find it, so i turn around and go back. he had a different sense of direction than me. when i go back i watch a thin man read a book on a wooden walkway over a small pond in the moon viewing garden. i can see the moon all day long, it looks frozen in the blue sky like a lopsided scoop of ice cream. it's the same moon i looked at last year, i think. i wonder if R is going to call.

in the meso american cloud forest, a man in a wheelchair is taking a nap. he is wearing the orange sun on his shoulder like a sash for autumn. it's almost thanksgiving. i am going to make an apple pie for sure, i decide. i touch the yellow bellflowers that look like bent wishes. L leaves me another message. it's about a dream he just had where we were in a back yard sitting on rocks and watching snow fall on the city. in the dream he tells me *happy birthday!* and i say i'm sad because no one is as weird as he is. *happy birthday!* he says, and i say goodbye and abandon him in the back yard. it's the same moon i was looking at last year and i wonder if R will call but i know that he won't. i get older and younger at the same time, wondering.

late in the night it's almost not my birthday anymore. i go downstairs to take out the recycling. it seems heavier than usual and i wonder what's in there, and what they do with all of it, and if it's true that nothing can come from nothing, and that nothing ever changes or disappears, it just changes into something else. the moon hangs fat and crooked, an egg dreaming of itself. when i turn to go back i notice a seashell sleeping in the shadow of the doorframe. i crouch to touch it, the wrinkle between my eyebrows deeper than last year, getting deeper still. because of things like seashells in doorframes, and everything changing into something else. there's a note on the seashell. *happy birthday,* it says. i recognize the handwriting as S. "thanks," i say to the recycling. i wonder if R will call. it's almost not my birthday. maybe he's looking at the same moon i am, but maybe he's not.

how to (write a poem)

let your life be defined by caesura—a break, pause, an inter-
ruption. in the case of your quiet clustered around moments of
rapture or shame, Proust had his madeleines, and you should
remember new york, driving downtown, the noise of everything
moving. you must have been very young, even if it was last week,
last year. even just now. here's how to do it: be very young. be
gauzily lit. materialize from the past. your poem may have a key
that's lost in its pocket, which will make you very angry, but an-
ger is autobiographical, so you can live there until you're very
young again. be either world-weary or nested, like a family of
dolls of yourself, each not quite the next. be open-ended. exile
yourself many times over. be quite small and unexplored, some-
thing of a darling, a lighthouse, a loose linguist—be a question
darting sideways clutching the pearls. flicker on your way every-
where. over here! over there. light all your little words from the
inside, this is how to do it. never aspire to "when in Rome" it,
never ever anything. set a little ladder but kick it away behind
you. burn right through the plumes.

in the heart of the heart of the heart of it

WEATHER

i had been considering clouds and then there was a woman on a cloud, a smiling girl with a scarf. she kept dropping her scarf down into the wind and it would twirl and fold on itself, inflated with grace, turning and falling and becoming something else. clouds are different shapes, and i get annoyed because they keep changing before i can interpret them. the deciphering of cloud-shapes is a position i could hold for a while, how a great white whale comes momentarily to blot the sun out, throwing the weight of its shadow on the flowers.

MY HOUSE

it's difficult to describe the bedroom, meaning it's not stationary like bedrooms are supposed to be. my aunt edith looked sort of like a turtle and lived on the other side of the stonewall, and she said if you get out of bed on a different side than you got in, you'll have bad luck. so i always pushed my beds up against the wall. one way out, one way in. every night when i climb in, i feel like i'm revisiting the actual scene of last night's adventures or catastrophes. the bed is like a backdrop. my bed is like a boat. my sneaky dream-self the pirate captain, she waits for my inevitable surrender to sleep, she raises the squeaky sail in the night.

out in the middle of the ocean once i stitched a patchwork heart onto the salty canvas, but it doesn't keep the sharks away. they'll find me if they want to. they make lazy circles and yawn, listening to my teeth chatter and the creaking of flimsy cotton, fruitless rudder, patterned with faded leaves.

A PERSON

when he shows up, he almost always stays across the room. i never speak to him except with my eyes, which won't be quiet. "be quiet!" i hiss, "you'll scare him off." but they don't listen. he smiles, or sulks, or looks away. i do something ridiculous and he starts to laugh but swallows it, his face turns red from trying. one time there were two of him, and one was mine. nobody could see or hear that one but me. i was very impressed. "don't be," he said, "i'm not real." when i realized him i was so excited with sadness i knocked the wind out of myself. deflated, i felt grass on my back and stared up at the blue sky for a while. he was reduced to a handful of little sparkling molecules of moisture, a glittering mausoleum, waltzing the air above my head. i watched him rearrange, then vanish.

CHURCH

two blocks toward the ocean and one block toward the bridge is an enormous cathedral. looking up, it looks like a church, in the middle it looks like a castle, and on the bottom, at the sidewalk level, it looks like a courthouse. the church is like a dream of a church and it's beautiful and it chimes the hour every hour. i can hear it from my kitchen. it's how i know what i just did and what i'm supposed to be doing next. i always count the chimes but they're always wrong, a little more indecisive than you'd think, for a church. i walk up the stairs sometimes, mostly at night or on rainy mornings, and cup my face with my palms to the thick glass eyes of its heavy wooden doors.

mostly when i go there it's like the church is sleeping.

it's like the church is sleeping like you might picture a mountain sleeping. breathing, heaving its big belly in slumber. a belly full of old wooden pews, musty identical books with pages thin as a film of ash, and lit candles. what would a church dream about? maybe women who walk with pigeons perched on the tips of each of their fingers. maybe people talking with their eyes closed. maybe a coastline of crumbled saints, a cathedral-sized hole to fall into. maybe the church dreams of itself washing up on the beach like a sunken ship. misplaced in history. maybe prayer-beads that speckle the shoreline like barnacles, or squirm into the sand and disappear like snails. maybe.

when i look through the glass it's dark in there, and cradles the feeling of having been scrubbed in hollow quiet for a hundred years. when i look in there nothing is ever moving, a big warm world of invisible mystics holding their breath, enchanted static, a spell is cast over the elements, soft-scuffed wood and colored glass subtled with smoke ring, mumbles, the soft indent of the knee in between its bones. deaf and dumb to puddles of morning forming at the shallow roots of my feet. when i step away, it always seems windier here than anywhere else in the city.

THE SAME PERSON

once i saw him sitting in the elbow of a very tall cypress tree, with a ukulele. i had been looking for him. "what the hell are you doing all the way up there?" i called out. he was swinging his legs like a little boy with a striped tee-shirt in an old photograph. "this is payback for your last poem." he called back, grinning, strumming, bridging two familiar melodies i couldn't quite place. i hung around and picked berries at the base of the trunk, humming, sulking.

MATHEMATICS

i jump at any opportunity for long division. it's what i like best. there is something so satisfying about bringing the next number down, raising the decimal. i mean, when you're full of equations that don't equal out. word-problems. the calculator is a good thing to test because the numbers keep changing when you look away and look back. where there was a one, there's a two. for example, if i jump and i fall instead of float, or if i can't see my nose while winking, and i look back and it says 1.111, what does that mean. it means numbers are imperfect, but still objective. it means nothing you've ever been taught is true. what that means is that the number one is the only one you can really believe in. believe me.

PEOPLE

or elephant seals were attacking cars and people were getting out to take pictures.

or a woman wrote a book like a treasure chest, washed up in the morning, the fog. seaweed and miniature clamshells dangling. a starfish trying to navigate chapters. or how when i sit on a bench, a toothless man might come and sit on the next bench and say i have positive energy, then lay flat on the bench and put a newspaper on his head, muttering, watching me read my book. if i leave and call my best friend in ohio to complain, she might switch the phone to her other ear and say, "well it could be worse." and she would be right.

ART

recycling sad like aluminum, glinting from this oceanic junkyard heap. it only seems to align itself as my ally under these conditions: i am a crumpled thing, on a shelf; i am trapped in a well; i am trapped like a tapwatered flower on the windless side of a window. ill-starred. asthmatic. waiting.

EDUCATION

i am maintaining a militia, partial to internal weapons that are neither concealable nor mobile. the local government is constructed of inanimate objects. the bookshelf in the bedroom is our president, it's where the only endings happen. we hold council in the kitchen over spider-cracked teacups, under the vine plants and pepper-grinders, and save the biggest decisions for last.

spanish for bird

i want to meet a man who keeps a clean, old paintbrush in his pocket. you know, horse-hair. featherdown. a man who keeps a pocketful of feathers. the tips of my fingers have gone missing, numbed by a certain empathy for pending weather, autumn and all that comes after, a certain picking-up-of-habits, nailbiting as a sign of solitude, sorrying, emotional wandering, taking out your worry and wonder on yourself.

i meet a man with a pink plastic bag full of bones. a man collects birds. reads me winged words in the way their feet are flung. once i found a green bird, the color of a perfect lime in a picture of a lime. flavor-color that sweet pucker on the tongue. a man leaves his window open all night. the pattering heart of a sweet-lime bird is flung into the sky and bursts into a star i get to name. i want to meet a man who lets me name a star. when i name the star i bite my lip and name it *pájaro*, spanish for bird.

i meet a man who worries that it's too late for chickens. "it's never too late for chickens," i tell him. the moon is in my eyes.

i meet a man in the dark. we sit on a green park bench, breathing giant quiet tree-air. a pirouette of fog lifts the sky away from us, just a little. lets the edge of a secret in, under a crack in our grass doorframe. i meet a man who holds his cards close to his chest. a man who is sleepy. a man who keeps looking at nothing in the distance. who puts his head on my shoulder under the streetlamp and sighs, as if we were lovers instead of strangers.

i want to meet a leaf-eyed man who whistles like flying, like slic-
ing the clouds to nibbles, pictures, brush the blue away from my
secret expanse of stars. exposition:

i want to meet a moon-flavored man who will kiss me on the lips.

dear,

water surrounds our city on four sides. like the ribs of ships. on every side ribs, which means the heart is in the middle. a reciprocal sea chest.

it was a bold move, quirky and unfamiliar. they meant to keep a respectful distance.

in neither case did the prose tart up to duck a poem's prettiness. by which i mean in both cases the prose itself was prismatic, fertile, berry-spilt, glinting this and that in both texture and scope. in both cases, i could hear you smiling, which sounded like low bells, three kinds:

1. a temple bell. soft, ringing. resounding. *right here: pay attention.*
2. the tinkling of bells on the front door of a hidden bookshop.
3. a warning bell, the kind i used to cinch to my dog's collar in the hopes that she'd inadvertently scare the porcupines up into their trees before she got close enough to give chase. by which i mean to give chase again.

it won't be long before you start to recognize the symbols. a yellow house with a wheel of green trees around it. a broom to bang on the ceiling. a bent penny you can use if you want but you can't bend back. a pretty box painted in flowers with a teeny ballerina inside.

i was delighted to see the tin, and the eggshell, but as for the book of love poems, i shall look out through its window like a planet looking out from its galaxy, waiting to be discovered.

"it feels like being internally discovered," i said. i may have said it to you but it's unclear whether you're there or not there so i may have said it to nobody. i was patching the holes in the pretty flimsy walls of a genre, the plaster drying too fast and flaking off my fingers like skin. i note this, ever pushing against things. something about my thumb the other day, pressing where, i can't remember. i'm sure you can relate to this shimmery line. a letter is a map. a letter is a trap. just your name pressed into my name with our invented geography spinning in the middle.

the eggs float, you said, as if in space, this world and all of them bound (as if) by secret knots, each knot the color of a different spilling. under another moon, nearer to another sea, a letter spills from a mailbox like an autumn leaf and into the silent street, which spills into other streets, and others, still. in this way one street is all of them.

wish

wish that lives in a thimble

wish that mumbles incoherently

wish that breaks the washing machine

wish that plays sugary music

wish like a noisy cup of coffee

wish that wants to take you camping

wish like a friendly bear who sits on your picnic

wish that surprises you in the dark

wish with a pigeon-colored story it's not telling you

wish with smoke tassle

wish that you crash into like an iceberg

wish you trip over in the dark and swear at

wish you leave out in the rain on purpose, then feel bad and
bring it in, leave it draped on the radiator to dry

wish with missing pages

wish that keeps writing its name upside down and backwards

wish you plant in the dirt

wish you turn inside-out

with that gets bright yellow paint all over you

wish you keep under your mattress

wish you write your name on

wish you write someone else's name on

wish without your name on it, not even one time

wish that challenges you to a watermelon seed spitting contest

wish that orders a pizza to your house from a different house

wish that rattles its bars

wish that picks the bone dry

wish that pulls every petal off

wish that careens around the blind curve while you grip the dashboard

wish in a driver's ed car as the student

wish in a driver's ed car as the teacher

wish *on* a driver's ed car as the sign on top that says STUDENT DRIVER to let everyone else know you have no idea what you're doing

wish that forgets to use the turn signal

wish that can drive better backward than forward

wish that can't parallel park so has to keep circling around the block until another wish leaves

wish you accidentally drop out the third story window when you're trying to squeegee the clouds off

wish with masking tape holding its glasses together

wish wearing a superhero costume

wish wearing its superhero civilian disguise

wish going undercover

wish in just its day-of-the-week underpants, but wearing the wrong day

wish having that dream where it's naked in a crowd of other wishes and the other ones are laughing

wish removing its glasses, wiping them, putting them back on and saying, "i see."

wish that escapes from a boat in another boat

wish that draws a mustache on all its pictures of you

wish that slips through the screen door while everyone is arguing and vanishes into the night

wish swimming underwater, holding its breath

wish and you braiding each other's hair

wish that gets drunk and throws itself at everybody

wish that always ends up being the designated driver

wish that loses the bet

wish that loses the marbles

wish that beats you every time at rock-paper-scissors by doing
paper-paper-paper

wish that spent all morning on the phone

wish with a pounding headache, hungover

wish on a bender

wish on the bench

wish that keeps a picture of you on its phone so it can look at it
in the airport

wish off the grid, living off the land

wish with a tin can telephone strung to a different wish

wish that yells your name out the window then crashes its truck
into the side of your house

wish that makes a nest in the rain gutter and then it rains

wish with a broken mitten string

wish like a wig that falls off

wish that tunnels out with a teaspoon

wish that can't find its other sock

wish that covers its eyes at the scary part

wish that never reads the fine print

wish that blossoms between two rocks to surprise you

wish that reads the last page first

wish that talks too much when it's nervous

wish that stops talking to you, and when you ask why, writes on
its notepad, "silent retreat"

with that would take a bullet for you

wish sitting on its hands

wish that prank-calls you, that when you say, "hello?" says
"who is this?" and when you say "what? you called me," says
"no i didn't, *you* called *me*," and goes back and forth like this
for a while until you hear its friends trying not to laugh in the
background and, flustered and embarrassed, you hang up on it.

wish that stops on the street and puts the traffic cone on its
head to make you laugh

wish that sings you to sleep

wish that waits for the beep

wish that drapes its jacket on the other seat

wish that shakes every cloud until a bird falls out

popcorn

Someone calls the radio asking where he can get duck fat or goose fat.

The Host, who is the ambassador to the radio for just this one of its twenty-four hours to live today, who is like the dog-walker for the radio and is taking the radio for a nice long mosey around the block, asks The Guest to share her recipe for Duck Fat Popcorn.

she agrees.

all the listeners look up expectantly for the treat, but with our ears.

if a radio is on in a kitchen but nobody is in the kitchen, does it make a sound?

"my husband says that this is what popcorn would taste like," The Guest begins, "if they handed it out in heaven."

how to read

1. poetry

sit in a living room and be bashful, debate a rabbit hole, and whatever you do, don't clobber the rabbit. funnel your autobiographical bunnies into a velvety blueprint, resplendent with etchings and accurate depictions of all the street signs, lamps, and umbrellas you've ever been kissed under. catch a lyrical glimpse of a slice of pink birthday cake with a crooked candle on a paper plate patterned with daisies. fold each memory of yourself being celebrated quiet and clumsy into an airplane and sail yourself across the wide, sunlit theater of someone's heart. let there be a pileup in the near-middle. friendly fire, gentle traffic. let them all discover you hushed, unfold you, smooth your creases one at a time with their delicate fingers to peek inside.

2. a field guide

let the bell ring, introduce yourself. illuminate your brilliant pit. belly. centered like a sundial, a fan of faces surrounding. imaginary. all your imaginary friends and their animals—pink pigmy giraffe, a galaxy of starlings, one comes with a snow fox who creeps along at her feet, curling itself through her ankles like a small, frosted creek each time she pauses, inhales, opens her arms wide to the sky and breathes forth a gaggle of tiny stars. let this be your tribe. let this be. loud, close, it doesn't matter, all you need is that bright seed at the center from which everything spins. you're a top. you're a point on a map with a tiny, pencil-drawn x on it. there's nothing else. you cope with grief at full tilt, and the bruise of your heart, like a back door, has a light over it. leave it on.

3. in winter

writing is full of drifters, and your heart's been trying to get arrested for robbing a bank. i mean a bookstore. i mean your heart's been sneaking up behind people on the wintery street, bundled inside their long coats and wooly mittens, and blowing cold kisses at their backs. their backs are dreaming of this under all the layers and layers of clothing, and your writing knows it. your writing is full of people who want to take their clothes off, but are wearing too many pieces and don't know where to begin. leave them alone together to figure it out. they'll figure it out.

4. a letter

emerge from the letter a day late and say, "what day is it?" to the first person you see on the street. they'll say *tuesday*, or *it's saturday, you moron!* say "thank you," and unfold the letter from its nest in your front pocket, read the first line again (*i can forgive anybody*) and close your eyes. it will feel like when you're sitting in a stationary car and the car next to you starts rolling forward and you feel like you're moving backwards. trust this feeling. say *dear,* under your breath, and fall back in.

5. an invitation

whatever you do, don't volunteer for submarine service. tell grassy tales, instead, chewing on a daisy stem, stretched out across the lawn of your life like a picnic blanket. otherwise, your conscience blossoms with everyone you've loved. otherwise, you squint against the burden of it, trying to find the horizon. otherwise, memory makes things look too nice. otherwise umbrellas. hundreds of them, thousands even, in april, adrift above your grandmother's crabapple orchard like a colossal flock of rain-spattered birds. bloom. *two strangers are coming nearer and nearer,* you should say under your apple-breath, picking petals from your teeth, *and sometimes they meet.*

6. a love note

do some rereading; adapt your focus. it will be a labor of love, a fictional soldier, your elegant dissonance, a symptomatic flip. pages whip through your fingers a paper love potion. find someone to drink some, then stand back and admire your work like a big-eyed visitor at a tiny art gallery. cringe a little when he turns to face you, his eyes filled with bathtub tears, scented with rose geranium, when you notice his heart steaming through his soft collared shirt, dampening the whole left chest, wonder if it might freeze when it leaves the room and steps out into the crisp, cold nights without him.

7. a growth chart

sometimes focus on mathematics. sprawling masterpiece, an infinite bristling. over the years (years!), your feelings will grow tall and slender like long-hearted giraffes, will develop patches of fur up top darker than the base, will grow spots and provide contrast. everywhere. some who undertake this get quiet or lost long before their hearts elongate. "how to ensure the length?" you'll want to ask the others. "what organ are you feeling for?" they'll want to know. you'll stop to consider this. your own body, everyone else's. *the liver that rinses,* you'll think. *the lungs that expand.* the right lung is heavier than the left. pause. "why is that?" they'll ask, their spotted brows suddenly snagged in a furrow. "if reading has any value, it's that it lets us in." *i know nothing about what it's like to be you*, you'll think. "the basic engine of any narrative art," you'll say, "is its capacity to puncture."

8. an apology

story your heart from a note-taking. have curious hair. with nary a lapse, be inclined to forgive. over the years, a bristling glimpse. someone will call you *emerging*, or *a tyranny of candied apple*, no one will call you mathematical. colossally disruptive. you'll be humble in your little red shoes and your finicky skin, but nobody will call you quiet, because your words will leap off the page and twirl sparkling across the city like sequined acrobats, like the poet says when he says. the first thing you have to do, you have to do by moonlight. make your fractal wish and hope for something to shoot across the sky in a telltale trail of sparks and splutters, storied into a discernable shape.

9. fantasy

spend all your life writing spells, tossing everything in the cauldron. snowmelt, loose-leaf, bird perch, horizon, migration, the Terrible Past, sleeping carpenters, caterpillars, sunlit kitchens, and all the fictions you can curl your magic fingers around. claim, rather bravely, that you read only because you love the smell of the bubbling. because you love the knap of the mountain. because you can only exist in its aftermath.

10. what you just wrote

you and your vigorous reimagining! okay, look. you have to clip it down. you have to pin. you're going to have to get down to business. i am trying to tell you how. listen: stop being such a saga. stitch into a comet trail, the next one you notice. (keep the chin up for noticing.) discern, mark, remark. no masquerading. show up nude. show up grinning. go to the city, tell yourself the story, again and again, and for crying out loud, know a thing or two. in the back of the bookstore, the cafe, the train, the river, sit unruffled in your cardigan sweater, fold your glasses on your lap like a napping bird with thin, dark wings, don't let anything hear your underbreath-hooting, what's that thing that doves do in the eaves? under the low-flying lilac? if you don't know, look it up. see that? the comet's tail is a-glitter. prepare to bedazzle. be a graceful but uncommon continent. let the bird perch on drapey telephone wires, ephemeral, forage for seeds on the floor (lilac or sidewalk, either way), don't let its long, drawn-out nest-call sound a lament. save your whinnying, your whine, shine, and wimper. let it wing a whistle like a flushed song. be here. right now. make peace with this.

flowers

abigail, the other day, wrote of one of her husbands, once he'd gotten old and become feeble and mild and apologetic, "he treated me like a flower." i marked it with my peony-pink pencil.

feminist or no, i think i've always wanted to be treated like that.

it may be true that all women want this. when i imagine telling Josie, who is not in a book but a bookstore, the one where we work, she becomes prickly and loud.

"noooooooooo!" she yowls. "because we're *not* flowers. women want to be treated like *themselves*. just treat me like *myself*." a man walks into a bookstore, scuffling his boots on the doormat.

"HELLO." she hollers from behind the counter, the door jangling shut behind him. he raises his eyebrows and snuffs the punch line.

but, still.

don't you want to be treated like a tulip? i want to know. *a violet, a snapdragon, a daffodil?*

my secret-self presses her quiet lips together, nodding. in her eyes this faraway-ness, this once-upon-a-time line of lime-lit meadow, winged things, where in the moon blooms its constant crumble to make more stars. in her lovely way of looking pulled apart by a question.

"*of course,*" that one says, her pear-blossom mouth softening for words to go by. "*petal by petal.*"

a new friend

september

a new friend: the guy from the census bureau. i find him one day standing very close to my front door, just on the other side, wearing a tucked in white-white shirt and spectacles without frames. some people wear glasses and some people do but don't, is what i'm saying. spectacles.

the census wants to know if i am interested in working 40 hours per week.

"not particularly," i say. i'm not wearing any shoes.
my new friend's name is MITCHELL. he snorts. i like this about him.
"me neither," he adds.

if no, what is your reason for not wanting to work full-time? the census says. *family? a medical disability? school?* i have a medical condition that can be disabling, but no disability. but that's not why. it's because i want to spend the mornings with my dog and my coffee and my pajamas. and like so much of my life, it's because of books. it's because ursula k le guin said `the unread story is not a story; it is little black marks on wood pulp. The reader, reading it, makes it live.` it's because i want to be the reader reading my own story to make it live.

"other," i say.
"other," says my new friend, clicking the screen.

he asks me to click my pay bracket for the last twelve months, and turns the census around to face me. the census has a square face, is very serious. i squint, scanning the numbers, hoping mildly for some sort of hysterical interlude, just to jazz things up i guess. the sky is a clear blue and the tall birches that line my street are fluttering their leaves like silver-green coins in the sun. my new friend sits across from me at my dining room table in his dress shoes. i'm not even wearing underpants under my pants yet and my own shoes are in a pile by the door like they ran in from a chase and collapsed. i just happened to answer the knock and there he was. now here he is, and the birds in the back yard are honking questions quietly to each other and their elaborate wondering drifts in through the open window in the den behind us like someone singing something under their breath.

"ugh," i say, clicking the appropriately empty circle with my finger, which makes it turn into a sort of surprised cartoon eyeball. "the worst pay bracket to be in."

"no, *mine* is the worst pay bracket to be in," says MITCHELL. snort.

"mine," i say. the census looks bored again, like it hears this all year long, blah blah blah, rolling its eyeball. i turn it back around to face him.

"mine," he says.

do you certify that all of the information you're providing is correct? says the census.

"yes," i say. "do i have to answer all of these?"

"yes," says MITCHELL.

"i have to eat rice and beans like five nights a week," i say.

"i have to ration my soap," he says.

"i do," i say.

"i do," he says.

i guess that means we're married now.

"don't tell him anything," mom says. i'm here visiting. she's chopping peppers and the old bowed plastic cutting board, always too small for whatever we're doing, is rocking around on the counter like a seesaw with every chop.

"can you please be careful with that knife?" i'm sitting on the counter watching, like i'm seven instead of thirty-seven.

"government tracking devices," she continues, shaking her head. "don't give him any information." she blows a lock of hair out of her eyes.

"i have to," i say. "he's my friend."

she harrumphs. ha ha.

"and anyway," i say, trying to make my most serious Everywoman face even though she's looking at the peppers, "the census is important."

"no it's not," she says. chop, chop. "what is he asking you?"

i think back, poking my finger into a pool of yellow sun on the counter, then tick things off like questionable decisions.

"how much i make at my jobs," i say. "how much i spend on groceries, how many people are living in my house, how sure i am of how many people are living in my house—"

"DON'T tell him how much you make!" now she's looking at me for a moment while she chops and the look is frantic.

"mom!" i say. "i don't even make any money—can you please be careful with that?"

"*he* doesn't need to know about it!"

"he's called me six times in two days," i say, which is like tossing a little grenade into a pepper patch and waiting for the explosion. she stops chopping and gives me a hard look. the cutting board tries to spin out on its weird axis.

"DO. NOT. CALL. HIM. BACK." is all she says: end of discussion.

i call him back on the way home to vermont. i might be going around a sharp curve when i do it.

"it's me, ali," i say, like we're old army buddies. i can hear him stepping out of the barracks of his job description and into the pumpkin colored leafy twirl of october i'm in.

"how many people are living in your house?" he wants to know. i laugh to myself. *oh, mitchell. he always wants to know this!*

"just me," i say.

"you didn't get married in the last month? still just you?" he seems to be making a joke, but it's hard to tell because the census is always in the way. i duck under some enemy fire in my heart (why are people always *talking* about this?) and suddenly remember i had a dream last night that when asked if i was married my response was *no, nor do i want to be!* since when do i say *nor*? just when i'm dreaming, i guess. and what is the big deal about getting married? either/or, neither/nor. are you *ever* going to get married? sure, when i grow up. when i get over myself. when i get left in the lost and found box like a missing mitten and another mitten finds me. but maybe when doesn't always have to have something after it.

"me and my dog," i add. i can hear olive snoring in the back.

will you be available for your third interview at this time next month? the census says.

i frown, try to think ahead. "the second week?"

"the week of the twelfth," he clarifies.

"well that's my birthday week, but sure."

"happy birthday in advance."

"thanks," i say.

how old am i, exactly? i wonder. at some point things became much less exact, but i'm not sure when.

the phone cuts out somewhere—wherever i am—but he calls me right back.

"hi," i say.

"you were in a dead spot," he says, and i'm not sure why he (or the census) is chuckling. "i guess you're out."

"i guess i am," i say, checking my rear-view mirror to change lanes, watching the long, gray road curl away behind me like a one-way magic ribbon.

november

on my birthday, MITCHELL calls twice. i don't listen to the message. he's called me every day, twice, for three days in a row. i am being november-appropriately peevish, petulant and difficult to catch. it's shiny outside, the low sun, thirty-eight years old, ricocheting off all the bare brown branches. "why is the sky that color?" i ask olive, whose nose is pointed down at something i can't see in the frosted grass. she thinks i am the sun and looks up at me thoughtfully. the actual thirty-eight (okay, 4.603 billion) year old sun is clearly shining but the sky is not blue. why? when it first came up over the mountain this morning, the sky was par-ty-dress-pink and surprising. now it's a non-color, the color of nothing.

when he calls a third time, i decide to text him to get him off my back.

hi mitch, i say. it's my birthday and i'm busy but i'll call you sometime in the next few days.
happy birthday, he texts back, then startles me with the balloon effect, a handful of digital helium-filled balloons in red, blue, yellow, and green that bob and float their way up the screen like captured dream fishes being released back into the wild.

december
i avoid MITCHELL for days again, but not as long as last month. the census always asks me the same questions. *nothing has changed!* i'd like to yell at them both. another new year coming, another trip around the same story. the same shoes i kick off the same way and that end up in the same pile by the same door. open, close. open, close.

maybe i'll go to the galapagos this year, i think, to see those marine iguanas. or to iceland, for the elves. maybe i'll apply to NASA as their imaginator-in-residence, planting everycolored flags on the mysterious interior planets of the mind. maybe i'll open a chocolate lounge, or a bookstore, or a storytelling school, or the door to an enchanted wardrobe that's actually a portal to another, better dimension.

when calling doesn't work, he starts texting me. i don't text him back, and then i do but i won't commit. maybe this day or that day, whatever, i say, kicking off my slippers.

are you going to be around? he wants to know.

maybe, i say.

just say when, he says. i can tell he's getting annoyed. "you're being
a little devil," says my grandma, in my head.

when, i say, and laugh my head off in the kitchen.

when you call

when you call, i'll be knitting a hat for an elephant. droopy, gray. gigantic.

when you call, i'll be making lasagna in a quiet kitchen listening to my voice in my head. i'll be just beginning my fall pledge-drive, trying to raise the vibe, or the roof, or the stakes. someone sad will call in and pledge their thirst or their art or their love, and i'll accept.

when you call, i'll be in the bathtub filled with ice. i run so much my legs are like lamp-posts. because i can't keep my feet still. because someone is always around threatening a game of tag. because i want to be faster than everyone, just in case.

when you call, i'll be writing a jacob-poem. a poem like jacob would write. or i'll write a matthew-poem. a leaf-poem. a dave or vaughan or tully poem. the only one who writes poetry i think is actually jacob. it's nice poetry, too. about sweat and love and loneliness. all these women.

when you call, i'll be sleeping.

when you call, i'll be eating a peach in silence. i mean slices.

when you call, i'll be trying, lying, spying on the doctorman in green scrubs who lives in the building next to mine. his bonsai needs water. he sets it on a paper towel and gives it a bath. looks at me funny.

when you call, i'll be peeing in the tiny bathroom, investigating my fun-house facial reflection in the silver faucet. my eyes are so goddamned big sometimes. no wonder.

when you call, i'll be banging out something on the typewriter. it'll say "when you call, i'll be angry. when you call, i'll be trying to be so angry," and it won't work.

when you call, i'll be a pacifist.
when you call, i'll be a buddhist.
when you call, i'll be a waitress. thanks very much. hope you enjoyed yourself. come back soon.

wishbones

eat the crust of your toast to make your hair curly.

since my hair was already curly, and i didn't want it to be, because mom always got the comb stuck in it and it was always in my eyes, i carefully munched my peanut butter sandwiches right up to the edges of the bread and slipped the curls of crust under the table to the dogs, who were always waiting for me to drop some part of my lunch on accident. a lot of times i did it on purpose. two brothers and an orphan, they had those big globey auburn eyes, giant long-limbed mystics, they were dogs of the forest. the swishing cinnamon feathers on their chests, their very floppy ears, their long, shimmery hair that swirled in ringlets when it rained.

if you sew anything on sunday, when you get to heaven you'll have to pick the stitches out with your nose.

it's sunny, and i sit sewing. pants are too long in proportion to my bottom. this is a problem. i never get new pants because of it. i wear the faded navy postman-pants with knee socks hiding my ankles underneath, no matter what the weather. in the sun i sew pants with pins in my mouth, little balls of pink and yellow and white poking out, a temporary decoration. i hope the neighbors in their upstairs windows can see me naked on the rug, bent over the sewing machine like it's a typewriter, a kitchen sink, a crystal ball. when i'm finished i'm never finished: i sew two of my fingers together. crap. bending my eyebrows i go to careful work with the seam-puller, hoping i am allowed to be all the time naked and whole, flying my cloud through the stars, when i get there.

an acorn at the window will keep lightning out.

i removed all the acorns from my window, why don't you come over. i removed the candles, snake plants, tailfeathers, and tuning forks. in their place, i put three glass birds. one for me, one for you, and one for the peculiar hybrid animal that is both of us. the sun glints through their thick wings and into my face, just before all the clouds turn black and turn my eyes off with a snap.

it's bad luck to open an umbrella inside the house—especially if you put it over your head.

my alter-ego is a stick-girl with no mouth named daphne. her face is oval and empty. she wears either a triangle dress or nothing at all. she is most often seen with an umbrella. sometimes it's raining but sometimes it's not, but she's partial to galoshes. she's always prepared for the worst, the leaves on her trees filled with apples shaped like ripe, heavy hearts that fall. the other day i was walking by a park and i found a wet slab of concrete on a sunny sidewalk by a white short picket fence and a cherry tree. crouched like a cat with a fingertip pebble, i carved her. holding her umbrella open. permanently mouthless and etched in the ground, expecting rain.

if you've been cursed, scatter chili-pepper around the house to break the spell.

little red flecks in my glass of lemons, glass of milk, glass of the window stuck open and peppered, i read it wrong and broke the banister, having something to hold on to was too confusing. the enchantment of contradiction. i live in a language of magic, that magical thinking of children, like if i say it, it will happen. if i close my eyes the windows all crack open and schools of fish swim in, birds like bombers, like drawing pictures on the sky with a magic marker. all my best crayons melted on the window-sills, the best desk drawer stuck shut. i've run out of envelopes or things to report in letters, lies, i've run out of reasons to look for feathers. they're everywhere. red heart-feathers shaped like miner's lettuce, growing down from the molding around the edge of the ceiling, the doorframes, in between books on the shelves. shallow water is scariest because you can see all the underwater things that swim there.

if you chew ginger, then spit it into a storm, the storm will go away.

i stayed home all winter long, pickling things. peaches, peppers, pears. have you ever had a pickled pear? they're disgusting. i stayed home all winter wearing every scarf i could find, wrapping myself in flannely wool like a plaid mummy. i'm a bear, i sang to the birds, in hiding. hibernation! look how colorful. some had stripes. some had fringe. i never did consider myself to be fancy. i stayed home all winter turning the heat up, wiping my nose with my sleeve, biting my fingernails. making fourth-grade tornados in pop bottles, watching the vortex spin on its invisible pinpoint, anchored to the cap like the moon. i am a woman made of water. i am a woman silhouetted by the sun, at dusk, on a hill covered hard and cold with snow.

garlic is a protection against shipwrecks for sailors, against foul weather and monsters for mountaineers, and against assaults by bullies at the local pub.

my mother calls and says, "old ships are washing up on the coast of oregon, but when the tide comes up in the summer they'll be buried in the sand again!" i remember to look that up, then forget. that same afternoon, i find a cameo of a forgotten woman washed up in the bathtub. sifting the bubbles i come up with more: a tortoise-shell comb, a cufflink with a pearl button, a broken black eye patch. reaching down between my legs i come up with a fistful of barnacles. i am all things salt, all things lost on the bottom. why? my dreams are jars filled with water. in my dreams i am swimming, always swimming.

eating parsley will make you lusty but wearing parsley on your head will stop you from getting drunk.

wearing a lilypad on my head (instead), i pinch my nose with a stolen clothespin, open my mouth big with breath, and dunk down under the surface of the pond. at that same moment, someone's nightgown falls off the line, is picked up by a wind and inflated, lilts a scalloped morning pattern off toward the forest, like a tipsy bird, a pink plastic bag, an april ghost. tadpoles rush away from me in all directions. lady-frogs tread water and lower their eyelashes at the whole living show, bashful, spellbound, enamored.

belief systems

something hurts. i call in sick to work so i can stay home and clean the house. i stay home to unwind my knee-sock from the string-taught roller of the vacuum cleaner, then i stay home to make up words, to read books that make me go to sleep. i stay home to wonder where i can get something better, something different, something i can have in secret with the sun shining in through the window making me feel guilty for staying in, as if i was starting some new religion, as if guilt wasn't the oldest religious trick in the book. i count words, featherduster, open windows and curtains then close them, and inspect my face in the mirror. my skin looks porous, doesn't seem waterproof, i take hot then cold showers and stay in there with my mouth closed, trying to prove it. i am my own science experiment. the projects that pile up on the desk, the floor, the windowsills, the ideas i keep in dusty jelly-jars with the lids so tight that i can't get them off when i realize how stuck i am.

i stay home scrubbing the cherry-red teapot with comet powder, scrubbing the splashes off. when i'm done, i rinse it and dry it and fill it with water, and it looks like snow white's swollen apple, that witch on her canoe under the castle. i was afraid of that part and of her nose that was so long and knobby and had a wart. i might be making that up, that bit about her nose, but i don't think i am. when my mother was a little girl and thought a witch lived under her bed, she was terrified of sleeping, and my grandmother told her "just don't get out of bed and you'll be fine." if i thought there was something under my bed when i was a kid, there usually was. the cat was in love with me and she would bring me all varieties of dead things to prove it. she wasn't water-proof either, every time it rained she was waiting at my window, sitting on the roof pawing the glass wearing a dead thing like a medal. this year i'll be twenty-nine and one commonality of all my years of bedrooms has been a bed pushed up against a wall. i've finally graduated to a box spring but never a bed frame, the bed sits on the floor and the weight of my sleep squashes any witches that might be lurking underneath it. i don't take chances. i stay home and chew my fingers, balance things on my tongue, talk to the dog telepathically. she wears a psychic leash, we both do, we have big brown eyes filled with sad and curious, we dream of chasing things we can't catch and catching things on accident. we never know what to do about birds.

i keep finding dead birds on the sidewalk. most recently it was a green bird, a sort of bird i've never seen before. the bird was the color of a lime that's been waiting in a pooled glow of sunlight on a white windowsill. i wondered if it escaped from captivity, if maybe it lived at the zoo. maybe it lived in a wire cage by a window in someone's dining room and the cat finally managed to chew through the latch. maybe it flew out the window just in time but was so disoriented when it got outside that it spun around in a panic of electric feathers and flew right back into the window. *smack*. maybe it would have been weightless in my palm if i picked it up. i used to steal newspapers from peoples' door-steps to scoop the dead birds up, cradled each one like a dead bird, a self-contained metaphor, but i stopped doing it because i didn't know where to put them. the trash seemed like an insult, and there's nothing natural here, i mean, there are little squares of nature, weird and soft and deliberate, and they checker the hard streets with green, but it's all backwards, like a prank we think we're playing on the ground. i mean, what's a lime-colored bird doing in the city in the first place. when i walk away from the fallen birds, stiff as stones, i feel guilty and relieved at once. maybe that's what religion feels like. maybe that's what it feels like to believe in something bigger than yourself, but you'll have to ask someone else because i wouldn't know.

i think i'm a painter, but i'm not sure. i haven't painted for a very long time, meaning years. i wonder if i've been disqualified for this, but there's nobody to ask. this morning i had the idea of painting a portrait of myself where i'm looking away and the back of my head is a birdcage with its door broken open, and a flock of birds are flying out. that might be when something started to hurt. i keep hoping i'll have a dream where i teach myself how to paint, but i only dream of swimming. i'd rather be a bird than a fish but i don't know how to choose. i'd rather be a tube of paint. i'd rather be a cloud pulling apart like a fish-spine. sometimes, when the clouds look like popcorn. if i'm a bird, i want to be in the forest, because when its blue is cracked open like an aquatic egg, the sky is just as scary as the ocean. i'd rather flit in and out of trees, nesting, singing where you can hear me but can't see me. what i like about birds is how they know where to hide. fish seem to be hiding by nature, so i could live underwater too, anywhere anonymous and quiet. maybe i should get a job at an aquarium. it's always dark and there's always swimming happening, swimming in circles. fish seem to have circular maps in their brains. a circular atlas. there's a possibility that i was a fish in another life. there's a possibility that i am a fish now, in some parallel universe. that would explain a lot.

my mother always cleaned when something was wrong. i've inherited things from the gene-pool that i didn't mean to. i'm reading a book right now about a man who can't stay put in time, he goes forward and backward and sometimes visits himself in the past. it drives his ladyfriend crazy, like when they're cooking dinner and singing "yellow submarine" and then he just vanishes, and she has to eat by herself. i sympathize with her on some level i don't really understand. it's like i'm the man and the woman at once, like sometimes i fly the coop of myself and leave her stranded in the kitchen singing alone where there was supposed to be a harmony. i don't really know what all that means but i think it's important to point out.

comet is hard to get off your skin. it makes your hands feel soft and medicinal for hours afterwards, but too medicinal like the hands of people who work in hospitals, or swimmers who spend too much time in clear water. the cat circles the bowl, waiting to make a new metaphor. the fish falls asleep mid-swim, hoping he has a dream of flying. i wash my hands, then wash them again. the dog waits under a cloud filled with birds, for something, stunned, to fall out of the sky.

love letter

if your breath was bread, when you spoke your ideas crumbled at the edges and left themselves, disembodied, along the wet driveway which was winding away through the trees. a leaf listed down the white sky like a bird. the bird could not decide which way to go. *which way did i come from?* it wondered. "where have you been?" i demanded, stomping my ruby rainboots in the muddy puddle's tummy. *i've been looking for you,* he said. he said it in a bright yellow way that shot through the hard heart of the colorless afternoon like thunder, an arrow, like a tender branch snapping from its tree and plummeting blissfully down to the soft, soft ground. nobody heard it, but it landed with a thump.

deconstructing flight patterns, hoping for the best, i had this notion of piecing a sailboat together from a number of small bones. caterpillars don't have bones, neither does the paper for a paper airplane. neither do larvae, opposite of nymph: noun: an immature form of an insect that does not change greatly as it grows, e.g., a dragonfly, mayfly, or locust. my statement is embedded in this question: what's with the birds? this is going nowhere fast.

i'm trying to deconstruct the projects. in threading things together, i found:
1. a lost girl trapet in a brocken hart
2. a cat trapet in a tree
3. another letter from my mother
4. "Haring Ibon"
5. what one can find when one was not even looking. okay, okay, i was looking. i had the binoculars turned around backwards and was looking at my other hand in the distance. don't hold it against me.

Maestro, conductor of my lungs, my feet, my heart:

in a dream i traversed the continent (wings of carefully balanced fiberglass, featherless, lit along the edges with electric candles, flicking the wind), wafting weightless down the dream-shoot (grandfather clock, a rockingchair rocking, my party-dress inflates like a parachute) i was only dry because i was standing on the tallest rock. a barred owl caught my eye. wounded, he perched high up in the aviary. a sanctuary. really? *he said some-*

thing to me i didn't quite understand, he said it in the eyes complete-
ly, in the eyes a sailboat made of bones, starburst flick of recognition,
or longing, or the fall of a gauntlet, or a don't stop looking, *or*
starburst |'stär-berst|
noun
a period of intense activity in a galaxy involving the formation of stars.
i used his starmap (it followed me / crouching like a cat) to find
my way out, or back, or in, or around.

the history of Home is holes in the sky.

the Philippine Eagle is the largest eagle existing in the world to-
day (tuesday).

he looks worried, his feathery brown brow, slant. in the avi-
an world, a Majestic bird. a Royal bird. they call him, "Haring
Ibon"—King of Birds.

there are sixty-four left in the world. *will you still need me, will*
you still feed me? an eaglet is born.

"Her arrival produced a considerable spark in the staff," they
said, "and indeed all winged creatures around the world. The
staff promptly named her "Pag-Asa" - meaning *Hope*."

stardust

i'm listening to an audio book and the narrator makes me want to narrate audio books. i google it, get some ideas. he doesn't always pause long enough between things, but his voice is deep and melodious, and i like his cadence, which means the parts of words he uses his mouth to point at. i've been keeping a running commentary of shiny things he says. i'm being like a magpie for ideas and how they make little weird looping bridges toward and away from my own shining actual body and me. a bone-map is forming. growing its own byways and lookouts and footpaths like an underground railroad for sense-making.

children extracting DNA from a strawberry, i write. *there are sandwiches in the secure room.*

the psychologist-author tells me (through the narrator) that my brain is 3 lbs of tofu-like tissue. that the cortex is the outer layer of my brain, and that its latin root means "bark", and that wisdom is applied common sense. if i get on my own side, i can change my brain.

"for example," he says, "most of the atoms in my body were born inside a star. how far back do you want to go? you're here because a lot of stars blew up." everything that comes together must also disperse, he says, but we're hardwired more for avoiding than approaching.

(is this ironic?)

"your brain is made of stardust."

my brain is made of stardust.

and another thing:
a lunchbox washes up with a diary inside. a writer (a novelist) finds it and when she opens it to the first page, says *print is predictable and impersonal, conveying information in a mechanical transaction with the reader's eye.* (a cash register, i think, an old fashioned one that dings like a typewriter, a transaction is happening!) the novelist takes in the purple looping words, twirling across the paper. *handwriting, by contrast*, she says, *resists the eye, reveals its meaning slowly, and is as intimate as skin.*
as intimate as skin, she says. *handwriting!*

as intimate as skin.

i'm so excited i text greg, quoting *Gone With The Wind.* "you should be kissed, and often," i say, "by someone who knows how."
he texts me back immediately, the blushing smiley face emoji, and then the one kissing the tiny heart, which i think is supposed to represent me, bright and red as a wild berry. since his brain must be made of stardust too, i hope i kiss him often enough, and i hope he thinks i know how.

how to (write a play)

flush yourself like a moon into the light. let so many soft spoken things loom but not large, perched right now on the edge of a nerve, making a difference. set a silent puddle of twists in motion with your tiny stack of clovers. let the mood in your head be whiskey, whispers, you guys in the back, dusting up a sunbeam, the black silk solo of your piners and perusings. be carried out by the band to re-create a texture.

learn songs for good luck soup and stumbling. write like a ping pong, a plover, like a librarian banding the foot of a new book. launch a talk to talk about it, this that and usually, write like the gesture you occupy when turning, when you illumine the layers, over and over. keep lists like little animals, peering out from the cracks between tasks. in some ways be cradling a funnel, finagling, but by looking both ways, preserving the gauge.

the play will be looking at you like you're just beginning to understand what the problem is, how to keep trying. let your hope and hanker hardly change, but when someone asks you what you do for fun, say "i break another leg doing the same thing i did, but different." listen to talk and moods and snaps and break words like stick candies, have an odd time trying. long to be coaxed, by a coaxing as elegant as a marbled memory, one as rich and studded with color as delicate fruitcake. you're a lot closer to a knock than a driving but someone has to drive.

knock, knock. hello?

what you want from a play is for the play to leave a light on, our hearts to flutter like moths on the porch when you drive us home.

dear,

i wanted to tell you something, and it couldn't wait, but i've forgotten what it was.

when i say i've forgotten, what i mean is the thing that's most important is that the door is wedged open. i mean, i'm peeling my way through your sentences, looking for the brilliant pit. waiting for you.

the moon, when it's out, is crooked. i'd rather us not be seeing the same one, but it's the nature of the moon to be always the same and different. there must be a word for this. i think the word is *library*. i think the word is *fissure* or *snow*, which means *falling in light* or sometimes means *a mass of flickering white spots caused by interference of.* it means cocaine, or dessert (*vanilla snow*) or a frozen gas resembling. if we use it as a verb it makes a bit more sense for us, i think? as in *to mislead or charm (someone) with elaborate or insincere words.* when it's flickering-white and falling by honeyed streetlamp, though—my god—it's beautiful. it's raining. it's january. in april, i hope you'll have come to your senses and stopped believing everything i say.
what i'm trying to say is *we're all starving.*

we're all walking chambers for buried gems, is what i'm trying to say. subterranean and dumb.
we're all being haunted by our memories, and hunted by each other's.

which reminds me:
i looked up your birth-day in my book today. the page was blank,

except for a splattered drip of someone's dark something, stained the paper. on the opposite page, it said,

```
he'd be invisible if it weren't for his blue
sneakers.
```

i looked up mine in yours before i left—i never told you that. the page was hypercolor, kaleidoscopic, it glowed in the dark like those enchanted plastic stars people stick to the ceilings of their kids' cluttered, canoe-sized bedrooms so they can sail their giant, winged dreams at night like galactic birds.
```
whatever it is that wants to be written can
use you to write it, it said.
```

i just thought you should know that it said that.

love, ali

escape hatch

i will never write a short, happy book called A Man Giving All of His Stuff Away.

this is a long awkward silence about getting lost and making piles.

there will be flowers that fizz up from the middle of the mountain, but you don't know that.

a mountain is a pile of ground, that's all a mountain is. you can read about it. sometimes it has snow on top and looks like a sundae. i look like a sundae or a mountain when i wear that weird white hat, or when in my mind my hair turns white and i stick a flimsy flower in my ear and it falls out.

when i am in a crowded room and am too jazzed up to shut down any of my sincerities, i will add but not subtract, then subtract, embarrass, retreat, travel to [another room], and start my day over by coming apart and laughing about it on the floor with the dog.

"you are the most genuine person i've ever met," a guy said, cringing, "and it's weird."

boldness of breezes, love of thumbs and spoons. love of being spooned but not of spooning. sometimes not.
he had barnacles in his mouth and everything he said was too salted. i just like to be the spoonee. but also to be facing the door. if i'm not facing the door then forget it.

love of the opposite of rubble, love of the fear of the theory be-
hind the first moon landing and all that math.

there is no opposite of rubble; the opposite is everything else.
is the moon the rubble of the earth? nobody really knows. i'm
wearing my smart yellow shoes today so i can think. i often trip
but never fall. i have two left feet, but then i sit down and have
no feet at all.

i smartly broke the moment. this, my area of expertise, the shim-
mering snap. i break it in half and when he looks at me like a
snack plate and asks if it's like breaking bread to share, i say no,
i still need both halves for myself. when? he says, but not when
what. whenever, i say. just not right now.

the bar has all these different stained glass lamps that hang from the ceiling. sepia-colored gold-rush photos of san francisco that hang on the walls. a torn painting of the old cliff house, which hangs over the sea. it looked like a castle before it got old and crumbled. a fireplace crackles by a dart board. beams. couches. wooden tables and chairs and mismatched furniture that looks as if it's been crumpled by generations of bodies, sinking down with a whiskey into heartache, or break, or warming, burn, felt words. you know. i love best the big lamp hanging directly over the long chestnut bar, fat glass flowers with round petals, all glowing reds and deep oranges and yellows and greens, lit from the inside. overturned-trough shaped. beneath it, an old man with a smoke-colored horse-hair moustache pours beers from a spigot and smiles into the dark. behind him, glossy rows of bottles, asleep on their shadowed shelves. i just finished explaining how three different young men wanted me to marry them. the first two are drug addicts now (downers and uppers, respectively), and the third was a joke.

"look what you did to them!" D said.
"were they always drug addicts?" L said.
"no," i said, "but they always had the potential."

it's L's birthday. she keeps smiling and calling herself old. we toast. "when i look in the mirror," she says, "i don't see the person i think of myself as. i'm stuck somewhere around twenty-eight. but that's another story." she is forty-two, beautiful, laughs with her whole body, and looks you right in the eye.

my heart is stuck in my body like a broken record. it skips and skips. a doctor (a stranger) is monitoring it, trying to figure out what's wrong, but i'm not wearing the wires because i wore them all morning at work. it was cold and sunny after days of pouring rain and everybody wanted hot chocolate. outside, here, in the bluish dark lit by yellow streetlamps and red tail lights, people bury their chests under layers and layers of clothing, and take most things for granted. they gesture to each other, slap-happy, laughing, and their voices make steam with their words, which push out against each other and coalesce, then disappear completely. from inside, they look like a silent movie. i name it february, getting older. it dropped down to the low thirties last night, and early this morning B said he saw frost in the park, frozen grass holding its breath for the sun to come up over all of our cold rooftops. the light from the stained-glass flower-lantern falls on us like something holy. i am thirty-one. i'm not wearing the wires, but i'll put them back on tomorrow. the tear in the cliff-house painting looks like a weird cloud, flesh-colored, like someone ripped a hole in the sky by accident, and discovered there was skin behind it. i look up at all of it, trying to know something i'm too young to remember.

"when i look in the mirror i don't know what i'm looking for," i say.

instructions for blushing

propel yourself by your wants, which are enormous, parabolic, starry-eyed, epic. note the element of surprise, your own blank loveliness, dove-like, the glamour of flying into yourself, or into him, or the amniotic unreality of making things up with some-one real you're making up. yes, you're allowed to thank each oth-er. tuck books under each other's hypothetical arms that spill out when you link them and puddle the letters around your feet. yes, you're allowed to gather them up until they kiss in a dream and wake up rumpled. soothed, confused, elated, sing-ing. when he writes from under his breath with his thousands of miles of wondering, listen from here with your head bent as if in prayer. flash wishes against each other from afar like flint. linger a bit, rubbing words together, then inadvertently burgle your very own story. take a window, a cloud, a rumble, nimble, and a few hours—maybe three. close your eyes when you lick the envelope. spend time figuring out a way to stop yourself mid-air, imagine those little USPS postal wings sprouting from your shoulder blades like guerrilla propellers and swing the whole bird around. dock in your heart of hearts, wherever that is, throw the barnacled anchor down. gently take the window from your duffel and prop it against the wall, press the cloud into it then toss a fistful of light to cross it out, wait for the glass to shimmer with the story's pulse. when you climb through, like water, hope he'll still be there on the other side, like a cup. if he isn't, lap up the moment of perfect lucidity (*this is it, this is what life is*) and start again, at the beginning.

letting

i 'misplace' traces of everything this isn't in handfuls and in my eyes, spread over the covers of the collected stories my heart zooms along, illuminated. they smell like the sky or dream like slipped jewelries to the floor of the sink in a silent clinking. they glint. some fizz. some are pulled petals and gather round, counting. i pop one into my mouth; it plays the trumpet fanfare all the way down.

some hints of everything this isn't might draw me a map that runes to the moon, or far and away from the dark space of illicit wishes between stars. i spill them from my outturned pocket, resplendent. a few of them start a pool to write poetry or protest Empiricism. two lean in, listening. one wears a stethoscope: *the heart thumps!* "hold my drink," one prompts another, beaming, and kisses me.

exposition

dear mister, hello. dear mister, goodbye.

5 things i am not going to tell mister:

1. i once was in love with a married man. his name was fernando, and he was flittery and embarrassed and had huge, dark, girlish doe eyes and he was always turning away from me smiling like he wanted to leave the room to smile in private. we all called him fern, as if he was the delicate plant which he both was and was not. in each of the few photos i *still* have of him, he is looking at the camera as if the camera is his mistress and it just asked him to do something that it knows he wants to but can't, and he's caught in the suspended sip of time just after he's realized it and right before the blush comes. the reason i won't tell you this is that when i finish a letter to you, the letter looks back at me this way right before i send it.

2. every night i go outside and hoist the sky up on my shoulders and stand there making wishes i'll forget by the morning. sometimes they come true but i don't recall ever having wished them down in the first place, which i think cancels them out. anyway the next night they're all still up there again, winking to each other in the dark like spies. i like that they stay up with the light on all night singing while i am asleep so i know somebody is keeping an eye on things because i definitely am not.

3. your poems are like snowflakes i'm trying to catch on my tongue. if they melt in impact, does that count as swallowing them?

4. how to get over our lights, stages, loops, lily-livery, the silhouette of someone who lingers in a doorway, which means the actual door is set aside so the way can glow around him. how to get past him. usually i send language slinking by like a troupe of kittens. one moment nuzzling your ankle on this side where you preoccupy with their wonder of shimmering whiskers and bitty paws, the next curling clean through your legs to the other, where they scatter like soap bubbles and vanish completely. poof!

5.

dandelions

martin bought a little yellow notebook in which to write bad things.

hardcover, with a sort of citrus peel colored elastic closure. "it's a companion to this one," he said, and pulled a little black notebook, identical except for the colors, from his pants pocket. his trousers, really—i think i think of martin as someone who can be wearing trousers. "i bought this to write good things in," he said. "but then the election happened and that was it for that idea. so this one" (the yellow) " is to write bad things in. it's—"
"ironic?" i offered, most of my face frowning.
(i have to stop this, i'm getting a very deep wrinkle between my eyebrows.)
"—better," he said, frowning back. "why ironic?"
i pointed. "it's yellow." really, it was very yellow. "it's really pretty," i added, encouragingly.
"yeah?"
"well shouldn't you keep the bad things in the black one? write good things in the yellow?"

greg gets on my case for saying should/shouldn't all the time. i read a self-help book once (i like to think of them as *self improvement*, since self-help sounds like *self: HELP!*) where the author said, "stop *should*ing all over yourself." kind of gross.

feeling thoughtful and overly chatty in bed the other night, i decided i'd start saying "it would be good", instead.
"*it would be good* to say that instead of *should*," i said, testing it out. "it would be," greg said. "*it would be good* to leave on time

for work tomorrow. *it would be good* to not hold your pee for an hour." i swatted at him. he laughed. "*it would be good* for you to be quiet," i said. "it would be," he agreed, smiling agreeably, shifting on my yellow daisy dotted pillowcase and closing his eyes.

"i was thinking of it more like caution tape or something," said martin.
"oh, okay," i said, disagreeing but wanting to be agreeable. "i could see that. i never thought of that."

i always thought of my dad as yellow. i mean, maybe his aura. when i was a kid, i just always associated the color yellow with him, like a crayon you'd choose to color in the sun. he never wore it or anything, i don't think he even has anything that color except maybe a flashlight or something, or a raincoat he bought for the dog, but he just always felt so *yellow* to me.

i don't think of it as caution at all. i wonder what this says about me as a person.

i think of it as a sort of clear, musical color, dandelions spotting the grass in the spring, suddenly, singingly, when all you've seen for months or can see for miles are a million spills of grey.

reasons for reaching

instead, i'm declaring my love for weather: *i am a window, look through me.* i meant to be a meteorologist. my foot got tangled somewhere in an unabridgement, a sharp turn of phrase near an opening to the inside, i fell into a bookshelf like a bottomless dumpster piled with whole planets of abandoned words and i've been trying to find my way out ever since. it's a lonely job.

-

a kiss sneaks in. a non-object. a non-idea. a round thing, a supple thing that moves as if alive. a slow, sinking thing with taste and sound and infused with meaning as if with honeysuckle, star thistle, water lily, lemon. oh, how i'd like one. my nose wet and lonesome as a wolf, cold, my liking funneled into an extra sense, or a non-sense, or i'm thirsty, can't you help me, as if i wanted to drink a lake.

-

dear, i'm trying to collapse you and me into we. i'm skimming the top of the pond for a good reason, a relativity, a resemblance. too much underneath. my reflection develops a tragic wrinkle when a frog leaps from the embankment to catch a mosquito. i must stop frowning. way down in wonder where my eyeballs are connected, contraction/expansion, where the room lights up with my best or worst idea. i'm hunting something, but i don't know what it is.

-

i'm very sensitive to cycles. what's the difference between a symbol and a metaphor? i'm an answerless, a guard crow, gaudy, purring softly in a yellow poplar, a Tulip Tree. i won't lose faith in humanity until we lose faith in flowers. our love for beautiful, useless flowers.

-

or catching beauty, setting a trap for it in the woods, like a brush-covered trick to disappear, teardrop steam, papery leaves down a slant autumn light, a rust-colored cheek gleams with sweat and salt and snot and all—

-

i'm haunted, lopsided, trying not to scare myself away. don't let me freeze my evolution or i'll be a sitting duck. all the choices we make are evolutionary votes we're casting, every single day. (you feel sorry for yourself, lips all a grumble.) harkening back to the mangle, i'm trying to know the difference between a zygote and a light bulb.

-

half-imagined dark things, or bright things, or skyward things. it's possible that we know as little about the sky as we know about the ocean. your guess is as good as mine. the world is brimming with invisible things we won't ever see. think about that. you're living on an island in the middle of it, your black eyes bright and glassy, like telescopes. all your raptures and sorrows leave you wanting, circumnavigate your self in a great circle, disassembling your ideas to more resemble saplings, wind, water. the way you want your lips to work but they won't.

-

"don't bluff your way out of your heart," you said, "but deliver the thing itself."

trying to fit it into the postal-blue drop box was another story entirely. when a sugary lump of it squished out of the corner of its recycled paper packaging and smeared genuine red against the open door, when most of the heart is hard, but middles are soft as fresh bread or butter, churned in the endless project of adjusting to the weather. it hardens from the outside in. there's hope for it. if nothing else, you can make breadcrumbs when it gets there.

eyes

i never really knew anyone whose eyes changed color until i met him. i mean, i know this is a thing, but i just never really knew it. my eyes are brown-brown. so are my brother's. and my mom's, and my dad's. i have a cousin with black eyes, like really black, licorice-black, but that's about as close as i've come to enchanted eye color, and we're not even related by blood.

when he wears his grass-green hoodie, his eyes are the color of clovers. when the sky is very overcast on a blustery january afternoon, a cool, stormy gray. sometimes when he's very close to me and his eyes make a little mirror for my brown-brown hair, they go a little hazel. but with a green fleck—like an acorn—they don't chameleon all the way just because i'm inside.

when he's in my grandparents' swimming pool, his eyes are the color of the blue-blue inflatable donut i'm floating in, where i balance my book on the kickstand of one carefully toweled thumb. "how are you doing that?" i want to know, his face suspended in a whimsical miniature on a crystal droplet of pool-water dazzling the very tip of one of my many wet (brown) curls. "magic," he says, his everything-colored eyes dancing, and disappears beneath the surface with a splash.

how to (write an essay)

if you're going to do it, don't do it on the basis of contemporaries, on the basis of the Best American, or mournful tales of butlers or swift, rivetless seams, the basis of Didions or Wallaces or silks or scenarios. do it on the basis of scones tumbling in their crumbs, of making a mess, mock irritation then laughter, secret treats, spreading the fresh snow down, hundreds of crumbs hidden underneath like tiny dangerous summits, delicate clipped departures. don't do it by addictions or devices, or dressed in defining garb, by worldly wardens or smart black sweaters or bristling with insult or trousers. do it by circling a square. by two palms of unfolding. not by donors or alumni, wars or whining, but by miniatures, wisterias, peaches and tiny personal crises sporting questionable spectacles. if you're going to do it, do it by your own spooky poignancy and checking in by checking out. by jazz and resemblings and polishing bells, bells, bells. do it by charlatans' burdens and autobiographical ballads, by alternates and adaptations, the secret sheen of the right pipeline. don't do it on the basis—do it on the range.

winter blues

JANUARY

january is a bad hat. pilly, the knit loose and thin. the hat is glued to the head of the year and if you want to pull it off, you can't, but another hat doesn't fit on top.

this is so dumb.

THE DEAL

the new president thinks climate change is a hoax. i think the new president is a hoax. climate change thinks the new president is a joke. so far, uncharacteristically, january agrees with everything—but neither of us thinks it's funny.

TELEPHONE

did you call? i saw that you called.

then why are you asking?

i guess i just wanted to point it out.

then why didn't you just point it out?

i just did.

AVALANCHE

january is a slow, sad person who rams their shopping cart into the tea display and knocks the whole thing over. when all the boxes of tea topple down in a little avalanche, january just stands there watching, sadly, and nobody comes to help. instead of picking up the boxes, january just turns and skulks away, head down. leaves the cart there, with a few piddling things inside that don't matter.

THE FOX

dear ali,

i've dispatched my fox—maybe you've seen him? in fact i've lost track of him. i have, in fact, seen him. just the other day i saw him, in the middle of the afternoon, crossing the street near my neighbor's house. he had a squirrel hanging out of his mouth like a peeled-off sock with a lot of tree-colored hair stuck to it. *i know i haven't been the nicest month this year. or <u>any</u> year? i know you curse my name at times.* well, that's a little drastic. *i know you've been taking baths and drinking tea and i know you have a sunshine lamp on your desk.* all true. *what i'm writing to tell you is this: i'm just doing what i'm supposed to do. i'm doing my best.* and then (this is my favorite part of the letter), january quotes john muir (!!): *"when one tugs at a single thing in nature," a friend of mine once said, "he finds it attached to the rest of the world." here's the thing: i have an important job to do. just like the fox has a job, the sun has a job, and you have a job.* and what is my job here, exactly? *please don't begrudge me trying to do a good job. i'm just being myself. at the end of the day, that's all any of us can do.*

  yours,

       january

finally, it snowed. hallelujah! i snugged into my little cross-country ski boots, laced myself up, stuffed my pockets with tissues, and me and the dog tromped into the woods, the skis balanced on my shoulder like twin pickets. when we got there, i realized every tree was encased in ice. while we skied, i cracked the frozen drips off the branches with my lanky poles as we passed, popped them in my mouth like winter beads. at the top of the hill, we sat on a rock and ate snowballs, which the dog thinks are fantastic delicate treats i make like magic from the frozen-frosting ground under her winterpink paws. we gazed out over the city, then the lake, to the mountains beyond it. the sky was up there somewhere, we could see little parachutes of it patching the mountains, white teeth of its light chattered across their divots and dives. down in the lake, the fish were asleep in a long blue nap, dreaming of july. january twinkled its eyes from the ice-twigs everywhere, melted in our bellies and came into a different kind of focus, slipped into a warm picture of itself as someone else.

NOTE

quicken |'kwikən | verb 1 make or become faster or quicker: [with object] : *she quickened her pace, desperate to escape* | [no object] : *I felt my pulse quicken.* 2 [no object] spring to life; become animated: *her interest quickened* | (as adjective **quickening**) : *she looked with quickening curiosity through the glass doors of the library.* • [with object] stimulate: *the letter's words— sunshine, fox, self—suddenly quickened her own memories.*

• *[with object]* give or restore life to: *they thought she was gone, but her body was suddenly quickened.* • *archaic* (of a woman) reach a stage in pregnancy when movements of the fetus can be felt. • *archaic* (of a fetus) begin to show signs of life. • *[with object]* *archaic* make (a fire) burn brighter.

A DREAM

i have a dream where january is knitting in a rocking chair by a giant fireplace and tells me what to do. "wear soft clothing," it says, "and read books, books, books, climb through the pages and pages of books into the nineteenth century into the english countryside where jane eyre saved a man's heart from freezing inside of him and expanding and breaking him apart like falling through a skating pond, solitary in a ring of thick evergreen trees, fast asleep and full of january."

"how do you know about that?" i demand, snuggling down further into the blankets.

january smiles and shakes its head, which sounds softly like a century's icicles clattering together, pauses mid-rock like a brown leaf suspended in a winter ditch, arches one white eyebrow like sailing a snowball at me in an icy arc. "escape," it says, "was invented by january."

TELEPHONE

i called january on the phone.

   did you call me? january says.

   no, i say.

you did, says january, you just called me.

okay, i did, i say.

what do you want? january says.

i don't know how to say this.

your hat, i say. i need you to take off your hat.

can't, january says.

just *can't*? i say. that's it?

that's it, says january, and hangs up.

THE WASH

i have to carry tissues everywhere i go. yesterday i nearly broke
the washing machine with them because i forgot they were balled
up in a rumpled clump in the pocket of the old snot-sleeved
sweatshirt i was finally washing. after the rinse cycle, i fished
out the clothes, which were like small wet blankets, using my
arms like fishing poles and my hands like clumsy cold hooks.
the wadded up bits of tissue spangled the wet clothes like slushy
rocks of snow. every time i sneeze, a river of muck bubbles out.
i blame january.

THE WORLD

january puts a sign up on a sandwich board outside The Public
Library:

COLD? COME GET A BOOK! YOU'LL STILL BE COLD BUT YOU'LL
HAVE A BOOK

it reads like a challenge. i can feel one of january's cloudy eye-
brows lifting, watching me carefully from its strategic position

(Everywhere). i decide to take a detour to see what it's all about.

there are two sets of doors to get inside The Public Library.

the first set (IN/OUT) is to slow january down. the doors are heavy and smudged all over, january having pressed its nose up against it too much, having breathed across it in an attempt to unsettle the library patrons with its incessant whooshing and long crusts of salt and dirty paw prints on the sad welcome mat of winter. there are two glass panels on each door, one on top and one on bottom. in the middle is the iron handle, which january keeps in the freezer all night and proudly presents to the sleepy town in the morning. (having come from a warm dream with woodsmoke and hot city council cocoa and little marshmallows of good ideas floating like tentative buoys, nobody appreciates it and january often feels slighted.) someone blew their hot breath on january and you can see it on the bottom panel of the IN door where a crooked heart has been drawn with a wooly, mittened thumb.

anyway, once you get past all that, there is a resting area before the second set of doors (IN/OUT) to get to The Public Library. the second set is to keep january OUT. between the first and second doors, in the resting area, there are rugs (january doesn't love rugs), vents that breathe hot breath down from the corners of the high walls (january actually gets smaller if walloped thus), and a large bucket filled with salted soil and a yellow plastic shovel. the man who uses the yellow plastic shovel has a voice filled with sand and string, and he wears a bright orange vest over a parka big enough to fit january inside once and keep it out twice. the resting area even has a long bulletin board along one wall. the bulletin board is colorful, and colored paper is one thing that works on january like garlic works on a vampire. i've heard (and it may be an urban myth, hard to say for sure) that if you wear squares of colored paper strung around your neck with plain string OR if you decorate your house with such squares by stringing them from corner to corner and especially along the tops of the windows, it will keep january OUT. january only likes grayish-whitish, sometimes with a little blue or weak yellowish (like old, watered-down dandelion tea) mixed in.

i make it past the first set of doors.

i rest in the resting area like i'm supposed to, just to be sure january didn't sneak in behind me past the heart-mitten window.

while i'm resting, i read the bulletin board like i'm reading a subway map.

YOU ARE HERE

the bulletin board says. i feel safe with all its colored squares of feathery paper, which overlap and jostle for position like peacocks in a crowded flowerbed. where did i come from? i wonder. **happy feet!** one peacock shouts, **therapeutic dance workshop!** she hops from side to side, shimmering her tail feathers theatrically.

i look back through the first set of doors (OUT/IN) to double check that january didn't make it to the resting area: it didn't.

across the street, someone has scrawled in lime green spray paint across one of january's sad, old, dingy-looking brick buildings: *save the world.* i nod once at january, who stands between me and save the world like a grumpy crossing guard, before heading through the second set of doors and into the warm palm of The

Public Library.

i made it! now i can really see what it's all about.

"good morning," the Head Librarian sings from the circulation desk. she has curly many-shades-of-gray hair with ribbons of bright white clouds twirled through and wears thick, round glasses that magnify her eyes gigantically. all around her, letters and short, dull-pointed pencils are swirling in slowly in wide hoops like halos with libraries for heads. strung from here to everywhere are more squares of paper. the card catalog spreads itself out across the stacks, infiltrating everything like a scent. the Head Librarian has a plum-colored nametag pinned to her canary yellow cardigan: MARJORIE. i smile sweetly, wearing my sweet victory in a healthy winter flush: january is distinctly missing from the scene like an ellipsis. MARJORIE smiles back with big, lovely teeth, old-paper-white. books beat everywhere like little hedged-in hearts, warm and quiet and full of stories.

"i was just looking for the poetry section?" i say.

"Poetry!" MARJORIE sings. her voice is like an april bird in a tunnel filled with near-flowers, and clinks against the library like a dessertspoon to a teacup, inviting poetry to kiss the other sections, such as photography, or travel writing. "third floor, north wing—by the windows."

"thank you," i say. she beams at me, her hair like a whisping ring around the moon, then returns happily to her work.

as i drift through the library toward the stairs, which twirl through the center like a maypole, i notice Two Things. the first is a fat man in a soft chair, reading a tiny book about sailing. the man does not look up at me as i pass, but his sail catches my breeze and inflates mildly. the second is a series of tall windows on the south side of the library, where the sun would stream in if it were summer, but where no sun is streaming. i frown at the windows, because outside, with its face pressed up against the entire length of the thick, insulated glass, is january.

goddamnit!

january.

BEFORE
when i lived in california, the sun was traumatizing. stricken with excess illuminatory stimulation [see note at QUICKEN], i was as lost as a glowbug in a lightbox. i had a hard time remembering who i am.
it went something like this:
i climb up inside the belly of the bus like a pilgrim.
"how much?" i say, "if you don't know where you're going?"
"well," the bus driver says, "where do you *want* to go?" he looks tired of going places.
"winter." i say.
"okay," he says, "you're on the wrong bus. this bus don't go any-where near there."

i climb back down, which is like being called in from the yard for permanent supper, like you keep losing the same puzzle, like an old man in a mountain, tumbling off the edge of a precipice in the blast of a last crumble, then doing it again.

i didn't know how to get from here to there, which means from there to here. and i didn't know then what i know now, which is that by here, i mean january.

TWO FROSTS

Jack Frost *is the personification of frost, ice, snow, sleet, winter, and freezing cold. He is a variant of Old Man Winter who is held responsible for frosty weather, nipping the nose and toes in such weather, coloring the foliage in autumn, and leaving fern-like patterns on cold windows in winter.*

<u>FAMOUS AFFILIATIONS</u>:
- Father Frost (fairytale)
- Snow Miser
- General Winter (also known as General Frost)

Robert Frost *was an American poet. His work frequently employed settings from rural life in the northeast, using them to examine complex social and philosophical themes. He maintained that a poem is "never a put-up job....it begins as a lump in the throat, a sense of wrong, a homesickness, a loneliness. It is never a thought to begin with." He spent his childhood in San Francisco but most of his adult life in northern New England.*

<u>FAMOUS QUOTES</u>:
- A person will sometimes devote all their life to the development of one part of the body— the wishbone.
- The best way out is always through.
- In three words I can sum up everything I've learned about life: it goes on.

yesterday i found a letter in my mailbox.

the letter was a little damp because of weird fog. here, where i live, there is something called the january thaw. i looked it up in the Farmer's Almanac, which is like the make-shift fifth grade classroom of the weather with grubby boots and mismatched hats and plastic colorful cubbies filled with extra layers and crumpled drawings of flowers, so i could tell you about it in more virtuous terms.

here is what the Farmer's Almanac said:

FARMER'S ALMANAC | Monday, January 25th | From: Weather

Related posts

- Curious marmot portrait
- Poll: Groundhog Day
- Bad Hair Day? Must Be The Weather

<u>What Is A January Thaw</u>?

Don't be surprised if temperatures rise soon. The days around mid-January have long been associated with the proverbial "January Thaw" when winter briefly loosens its icy grip.

But what, exactly, is a January Thaw? Is it real, or just another weather myth?

The January Thaw, like Indian Summer, is more than just another piece of fanciful weather lore. Annual averages really do show a slight temperature increase, and subsequent dip, during the final week of January.

this explains the dampness.

anyway, i reached my mitten into the mailbox, which was like a small, metal cave that might be filled with bats in the back. instead of bats, what came out was one community newspaper with a grainy cover photo of smiling people wearing sweaters, one flyer with four discount pizza coupons, one maple key that had somehow lost its way from october, or maybe had been hiding in the mailbox waiting for april (i unhooked it from the newspaper and threw it back into the mailbox's creek) and this damp letter. guess who it was from?

i gazed out across the street toward the mountains in the distance, in their thin snowsuits of lavender and lilac and soft watercolor winter shadow. i wiped my cold nose on my mitten and carefully refolded the letter, tucking it back inside its damp envelope like i was folding an ancient napkin to dab at the woes of the world. my dog looked up at me from the icy mailboxy median with her snow-white eyes, deep brown irises in the middle like fertile flower soil, the alternating bands of gray and white sky reflected there like lace doilies set under warm cups of dandelion tea.

"january," i said out loud. my dog's name is olive.
"january," she agreed, with her dandelion-eyes.

i'd already started preparing my response, where i would shake my mittened fist, demanding to know what, exactly, i was expected to do about all of it—and then, the most miraculous thing happened.
something came unstitched in the cloudhat, and there (right there!) in the part, where the thick silverwhite hair of january flattened away from itself, was the bright blue head of winter.
"it's still there!" i yelped, finally understanding my job.

blue, blue, through. my job is to notice. this is the only way.

listening for january is like sticking your soft ear in a dried up, sky-bleached conch shell and trying to hear the distant way-ward sea inside. there are snow people, of course, who stare into cool space with their pebble eyes and sing branch-and-scarf songs about little sisters and icicles and plastic sleds and buck-ets with the corners cracked. they wear dingy cherry hats and have vegetable noses that, in the night, the fox admires in the cloud-blocked moonlight under an elaborate suggestion of stars. listening for the fox is like listening to january and its crystal music. everything is stuck awkwardly in the snow. the best mu-sic for january is baroque piano. i dance with the dog across the living room with all the lights on in the middle of the day, and we pretend we're in a royal court to entertain the queen of winter, or we're just silhouettes on a swell of snowcapped hilltops, every step crunching into the belly of january and leaving little jewels of sapphire ice in our paws and boots and sparkling us further into our cold, clear, wintery song.

dear,

this is a list of everything i'm going to need you to be.

last was never the place to meet. but what should you *do*? yank open your winter coat, sending the buttons sailing across the room as a series of pops into the fluffy asparagus fern? put your nose to my neck? okay, no, don't do that. movement is always beautiful, but—still—don't.

you can read this letter as you would any other letter. it's been said that *struggle changes an ordinary human into a spiritually awake person.* (no, you can't read this letter like that, can you.) read it like this:
a herd of elephants eating cashew leaves and singing.
or this:
your mother had a dream when you were buried in her belly. deep well, brilliant sunlight.

the dream may have had three heads, like that terrible dog of the ancient underworld (you know the one!) and they all had eyes for only you. i'm going on a picnic and i'm bringing a deep well, brilliant sunlight, and a flat rose trellis painted up the wall of our meeting. if i write you a letter, you'll have to meet me here, because your conception was the letter your mother wrote you and you responded.

forgive me for being forward, but tides do turn, sir.

you have to start sometime, you said. i'm almost certain you said this.

i'm standing here with my little stick, attempting to draw a line in the mud for the sake of you.

love, ali

versions

then we lay like that, tribal, warm-blooded, having hooked our limbs like celtic knots, in our frenzy where our breathing is bellows, where we smell like animals. composure unravels like a bandage, a kite string. we unfurl like flowers.

i uncrumple a newsprint flower, peeling the inky text away like the skin of an orange. "if i was an animal, what kind of animal would i be?" it says. the ink smudges my fingertips like ash, oily, inside the crumple it's warm to the touch. you look out at me, glint where i tilt you to the nightlight. dust to dust. a whole hidden mythology, spilt across the eyes.

"your smell," he says. "i do?" i say. "i missed it." he says. "oh," i say, "that's not what i thought you said."

"i make love two times," says the guy behind me on the bus. to *time*? to *hide*? what did he say? someone must have squeezed his voice from his throat and stretched it like a caramel, scraped it over the asphalt, pockmarking it with little

rocks, slivered by a crack in a downtown side-
walk. you know him. midmorning Banter-Lis-
tening, Bus-Riding Alone. we all are.

or, please don't open me near the sink. i don't
know how to swim.
"you're good at that," he says, unspooling the
space between us down his chest, his belly, be-
tween our skins, our eyes. mine are like teacups,
a tea-party, pocket roses. saucers ladled with
milk. his are towering pine shadow, rain on the
forest floor, dark pools darting secret minnows.
i tell him everything i know.

these: bone against skin, knuckled, calloused
from digging dirt under winter rainweight, lift-
ing stones pocked with muscovite or moss, hard
under supple, naturally occurring weaponry
that swells up from the ground. i feel a little
sick, my mouth and my mind mismatched, i lick
my lip, backwatering him, tasting oranges.

i'm a tired-of talker with sleepy-eyes. dayafter.
my mysterious dream affairs with water: i seem
to be the cat and the goldfish, lonesome figh-

terfish, scrappy tabby, tailed, striped, circling
the bowl. on the bus a man gets on and says,
"i think she's been talking to me in her sleep." a
girl is left on the corner, is wearing hair in her
eyes, like glasses.

winter fountain spray of white, a spray of baby's
breath. pressure and air makes the same amount
of water more. thirsty for its plural form. i'm
so sleepy, my head nods about, eyes flying half-
mast. my conductor of dreamwater, fruit parts,
a greenhouse, i think and think and look and
grow a spare heart. a man cradles a clementine,
his hand the color of cardamom. another has
breadcrumbs, is the center of a sundial of pi-
geons. thirsty to be at the center of something, i
balance an orange pencil on my lip and make up
things for our eyes to be.

a man on the bus falls into another. men being
softer than they think, they both bruise. a soft
spot in the skin to sneak a worm, or a tooth, or
a secret.

words rub up against me: it's not enough. i

bite my lip to keep from wincing my voice out from my trappy throat. "a bird throat," he says, smoothing the feathers down. i'm writing a play where he's the only character, playing himself. a different animal plays him in every act.

in one version of you, your fingers always smell like oranges. you unwrap it delicately, tap a fracture in the peel, crack it open like an egg. there's something alive inside.

warm-blooded. freckle-back down. he sleeps. i inspect his profile with my dream vision. i'm wearing my dream glasses. the morning is color-scented. he has tiny, sun-colored hairs coming out of his ear. what kind of animal are you? i'm looking at him like a farmer. the room goes apricot and i go kernelled, hourglass, above-water, i'm belly-up watching his jugular inflate and deflate. i guess his heart does that. "do you float?" it asks me. "i do," i say quietly, holding a flower in my teeth, not knowing how it got there. suddenly i'm a little lost, somewhere between one edge and another.

it's too much, it kind of hurts. a pulsing knot, arms and legs sticking out. if only i could slide out of the mirror of skin i'm wearing, leave my exoskeleton in our tin-can rosebush, rusting along with history. i could rocket myself to the moon. "*fuck*—" i say, instead, like it's the only word i know.

nerve

today i'm throwing a tiny colorful tantrum at my imagination. i'm taxiing the tantrum around like royalty and letting it do the queen's wave from the window, wear a fascinating hat cluttered with play pearls and feathers. my tantrum is getting a blister, needs to put its feet up. its left feet, all two of them. i let it sit sideways to try. the world presses its nose up against the window, banging on the glass. my lungs are filled with words instead of air but i'm somehow not drowning. or i am, you are.

i press a button that says DO NOT PRESS so there's something about you that sneaks up on me. it either breathes against my neck or pulls me hard back against its chest, pressing most of my own breath out to lace yours through. it's like holding hands but the hard way which is the only way i like. sometimes i like the feeling of being smooshed and other times not because i can't breathe even though sometimes i love the feeling of taking a very big breath and holding it forever. first it's like being under water and then like at any moment i might lift off and float away to be rinsed by sky like a bright balloon. when i let it out i can start over, okay?

pinprick, pop, free fall, the difference between the pink balloons and the blue ones. black ones. the black ribbon at the wrapping station is always fully spooled because nobody uses it even though some small part of everybody wants to. like on some days when we're the bead of light in the dark pool and others when we are the pool itself, but look! there's a sparkle on the far side and let's swim to it. the swimming shimmers back and forth like birch leaves which look like silver dollars, but stolen, cinched, and flickered in the wind. but who is breathing down whose collar? breath too bright to tell, we don't know. or maybe we do but i don't.

i love this rustic rustle and i suck it up like a song. i do the move, my signature move, where i stomp my foot turning, each stomp a click of the turn like a clock. i get all musical. what my time/ your time is it? the tantrum is because they're different. it fizzes up my fingers and out the tips like eyelashes and i use that to electrocute my itches. not like they need it. they're the reason i throw things in the first place, the reason the wall of my whatever is spattered with fusses of color and winking lights and the infuriating mystery i keep trying on that is you or me, that i keep putting on my head or tucking behind my ear like a match, or a flower, me or you? but it's my own ear after all, so the itch must be you. and me.

but mostly you.

hanging from the sky,
swaying with the bee-moons happy
(us): Hafiz

not knowing where to start, i start everywhere. when i ask H, he has only nonsense to offer.

"i think we need a password," he says. he is pointing at me with both index fingers. both of them.

"for what?" i say, not looking up from my book. he sits on the other end of the couch, not-reading, not-straight, and certainly not straightfaced, facing me.

"because then when someone—or even a story, or a poem, an idea—came up to the window wanting to be let in, we could shout *tell us the password!*"

when i close my eyes, there are slices of light like bright lemons behind them. i wonder if he is doing this or if i am. something sweet and startling. we are sitting on the couch in the picture window. the not-so-distant mountains are steady and indistinct, watercolory, meadow-green, maple candy-colored, periwinkle.

"—or even a BIRD!" he says, opening his arms and eyes as wide as wings.

now it's my turn to point at him.
"don't do it," i say.
he grins.

"don't."

"don't do what?" he is fishing. a bright, feather-glad lure tapdances across his eyes. he does this. it's like he always wants us to be putting on a play. we both play the one who speaks directly to the audience, and everything (everything) else plays the one who doesn't know the audience is there at all.

"the *irony!*" he says.

"you know," i say.

the world is perched at the edge of its seat.

"did *you* know," he says, his bright eyes narrowing, "that the space above the stage in a theater is called *the flies?*"

he's not going to do it. maybe we can have a quiet morning after all. after last night, it's all i want, really. i turn back to my book.

"the night sky *sways* above us like a blank handkerchief!" he cries, clutching his head dramatically.

"i don't like flies," i say. "and H, it's seven o'clock in the morning."

"of course you do," he says.

"come on!" i say.

"what are you reading?"

sigh. i hold it up.

"*The Art of Memoir*," he reads. "ah!"

"what, 'ah'?"

he looks smug.

"*self-satisfied, complacent, superior, self-congratulatory, pleased with oneself*, etcetera, etcetera," he says.

"cut it out!"

"cut what out?"

"you know!"

"i want to be in your memoir." he leans back, crossing his arms and looking down his long nose at me.

"you already are!"

"what does she say about TRUTH?"

"who," i say, "Mary Karr?"

he nods, suddenly solemn.

"a lot. it's about memoir. it's kind of a memoir about memoir."

"a *memoir* about *memoir*..."

"kind of."

"is that what you're writing? a memoir?"

"no. i don't know."

"is it TRUE? what does she say about which of your friends to include?" crazy eyebrow-wiggling.

"chapter twelve," i say. "*Dealing With Beloveds (On and Off the Page)*."

this elicits a whoop.

"BELOVEDS!" he yells, throwing his bird-arms open to me once again. he flutter-waves his hands around, for once not finding words. "THAT'S US!"

i laugh, in spite of myself, because of course he'd react like this. he is like an orange-robed bird of paradise. those ridiculous beautiful dances they do. their bizarre headfeathers. their calls like short-circuit radios, floating bells, dream-speak. in their colorful longing to connect, to be seen, to belong, singing their flying hearts out for all of us.

advice column

dear Starting Over,
think of caterpillars. hedgehogs. carrots. while gardening, imagine a world without dead people. say sorry about yesterday, the rest of me lacked. it's all been blessed by the bloom. i mean the electric glow, i plugged it in. plant over it. the lack of love in life. the look on everyone's face. evidence in favor of the world being on your side: flashlights, birthdays, phantoms, strawberries.

dear Bewildered,
methods of temple, the hammer used is laughter. i mean light. suddenly he finds it in the pocket of his coat. his hair is like paper curling at the edges. sugar-apple white, pain, icebergs, magicians, none is more effective than language. (even a kick to the cypress in the courtyard!) intending to realize the way opposing the way, all we need to know is this: to point out the moon, we must use the finger, but we must not mix them up. the finger is not the moon. mountains are mountains. lampshade, umbrella, same thing. try being the crystalline heart where the earth cracks and converges, or possibly the lamp itself.

dear Leap and The Net,
pass like rain from place to place, like a pink city-moth flutter banging herself against an embrace of tinsely light, the busy bedazzle of a fancy horizon. accompany yourself on purpose, like the second handful of high notes on the piano of your next best

move. i'm telling you it can be done! chaos aligned, the bird
in the margins, a shiny dodge, orientation of light. a pale flick
and swell, honeycomb of sleep, work the inner electrical until
your heart runs high. we'll feast in tumble chambers, luminosity
shamble, star-streamers, a cheery sniffle, watching the bald sun
galloping just beyond where you assumed the horizon to be. tell
him what in an unmuffled buzz, no garbling, no polishing rags.
look him right in the face and say, why does even the air seem to
start with your eyes? once upon a time it. kick it off.

dear Looking for A Lifeboat,
escape a curious distance. tap a little pencil, the kind you get for
mini-golf. choose the creamy pink ball, let someone else have at
the red. describe trees and captains as being so young and grow
your promises like pearls in a shell or pull them from thin air
like magic tricks. once upon a time there was a bird, start like
that. develop a gentle respect for burying the seeds. when you
bear fruit reason your flowering with the absolute clarity of a
two-way temple. talk to yourself in your head. say hand it over,
it's not a necklace. say it's time for bed, close your eyes, they've
been open all day. be a world-class cook in the kitchen of your
mind. in other words, don't go crazy, but always exist, always be
young and reading. and running. and lovely, ballerina your way
out or in, a kind of habitual-twirling, opening a cloud of flowers.
allow yourself to be abducted by stories, arranged whimsically in
a matchbox, a teeny version at the end of a taper, hypnotized, in
a state all your own. blink the stars on and off, be a museum at
night, live in a secret cradle of light. say at least this is all true.

at least the length of the light is longer, acorns and oak leaves woven in, fresh as a glass of water in a spring window. suck a milkshake through a straw. put your feelings into words then back into feelings. feel like a paperclip in a puddle or a squirrel in the rain. feel like your own fragile nature. put all of this into words; say there are so many clouds i don't know what to do with them, then sail away on one into the blue, blue, blue.

dear Messy Directions,

sally forth until you no longer know, or think up under your skirt like a secret flaunting itself gorgeously, like singing in pajamas. reach over and touch a ribbon, blinking, pull over, bring an idea to your lips like a candle and blow it out. picture the demons at work then make a theatrical show of uncrumpling and smoothing them, accepting their apologies and telling them not to worry. push things a little too far. climb into the cartoon of your life and start saying things like, "yes, can you tell me where i am?" or "it's important to note that at some point i turned out to be a variation." compose variations on a theme. snails, for example, or hearts or fields. when someone, concerned, asks you what exactly you're saving in your savings account, say i'm saving a space. if they ask where the one thing ends and the next thing begins, say there's nothing here that says you can't move the fence.

dear Happily Ever After,

have an opinion but not all the time. stop worrying about zebras, films, drawings, coffee. buy your own damn drinks! build

a bridge but cover it with sparkling ice. uncrumple your jack-
et from your body. imagine the girls can't see you. happen, and
mean it. mean it even before you happen. cushion, cover, mea-
sure, need. let your heart burst but not all at once. whenever
someone asks you if you are, say "i might be." feel infatuation or
don't feel anything at all.

dear Tiny Revolution,
render a hodgepodge. pucker, panic, and poppy. go for croco-
dile-petaled, but don't be plucky if you're underwater, and please
don't yell at the jellyfish. lettuce window, pink project, open up
for a few days then try climbing the sky to the moon to see what
the moon might do (mind its own business, pretend to be a para-
sol, etc.) it's not as exciting as becoming, but everything is be-
coming anyway. becoming means blooming because it happens
in a loop. trust this. write it in the steam on the mirror to remem-
ber then forget again when it disappears.

dear Tempted,
sharpen his name like a pencil then fold it up in tin foil and put
it in a drawer. pretend he's a tooth that fell out of your mouth,
that you grew out of but blanched and bleached to keep it. when
someone calls his name look up like they called yours. pay atten-
tion to color and the way that frost can crack stuff. when you re-
member and a little light flies out snatch it, pop it in your mouth
and swallow it. it's nobody's fault you threw yourself into the
pond and found a frog. why are you always kissing everything?

wake up and kiss the world instead by waking it. orchestrate a flood that turns twice, carries you away together. if that doesn't work, invent a moon for yourself and—weird—it looks just like him. plug it in but turn it off. if it doesn't work, turn it on and then off again.

dear Bashful Extraordinary,

perch like a preacher at the top of a song. lose your name in the leaves. feel like a fern unferning. don't pretend you're a flower if you're a flower. keep an ear out for color (iridescent duck-dark, butterfly crossings) and a cup out for ideas (peach pits, moon passes, cold crackling the jelly jar in the yard). when you open your arms, light spills out and everybody will have hallelujah eyes and the path will be illuminated. when you close your eyes and send yourself off in the dark to walk through puddles and the puddles are filled with music, by music mean frog songs, and hold still to listen. by everybody, mean everything. by frogs, mean stars.

on sleep

i am traumatized by sleep, my family has the worst sleeping habits. my mother falls asleep everywhere, in cars, on benches, couches, once in the Louvre in front (i'm not kidding) of the Mona Lisa. but she especially falls asleep on a chair in front of The News, her soft ears catching half the night on jagged bits of disaster, panic, global chaos, threaded anger, clotting her dreams in little fisted knots of alarm and unease.

"how can you sleep like that?" i want to know. "why don't you want to go to bed?" i want to know this for thirty years. why do you try to keep watch all night?

"i do go to bed," she says, aghast.

"at 2am? after you've been sleeping upright since 9?"

"so what? why does the time matter?"

"you get up at four in the morning," i point out, "and have to drink an entire pot of coffee. you're exhausted."

"okay ali, " she huffs, getting annoyed.

"it's because i care about you, mom."

"you do your thing," she snaps, cat-cornered, "and i'll do mine."

because of this, i have issues around sleep and sleeping. "it's always the mother's fault!" she likes to say, but it's not your fault, mom. everything doesn't have to be somebody's fault. either way, i have rules, boundaries, and elaborate bedtime rituals that, when interrupted, make me cranky and, at times, throw me into a mild and wholly irrational panic. i turn all the lights down after dinner. i take a hot shower in the dim bathroom scrubbing myself with warm soapy minty suds, rinsing the day away. the sheets must be clean, the bed having been made neatly in the morning and left undisturbed until bedtime. the room should be cool, but the blankets heavy. the pillows should be on *top* of the blankets, but nothing (*nothing*) must ever touch them except for my head—or greg's, but only his own pillow for his own head. sometimes when he comes over after a long day of work and his feet hurt and i'm upstairs doing yoga, he flops down on the low bed to keep me company.

"OFF!" i yelp. "get off of there in your street clothes! *the sanctity of the bed!*"

he rolls his eyes upward, then his long body over and onto the nubbly carpeted floor with a hushed thump. outside, everything is purplish, a northern winter four o'clock bottom of the sea-ish.

he drops his two coins in to see what he gets.

"i'm not dirty," he tries, belly-up on the rug like a stranded starfish.

"yes, you are." i say, not having it.

"i took a shower this morning."

"no."

"my clothes are clean!"

"..."

he groans, but is mildly amused or mystified or both at these bizarre antics that he doesn't completely understand. he gazes magnanimously up at the creamy pebbled ceiling that i've already rinsed with my imagination in an oceanic dazzle of friendly stars for later, sighs.

—

mom used to fall asleep in the parked car, in the garage, when
   we'd get home. "just leave me here for a minute," she'd say,
   waving us away like fruit flies and putting her forehead down
   on the steering wheel. we'd run inside to raid the pantry and
   play with the dogs and turn on the tv and watch *Night Court*
   or *Cheers* until dad came in from The Library where he'd been
   working on who-knows-what-probably-doctor-stuff at his
   desk.
"where's mom?" he'd ask.
we'd shrug like synchronized swimmers, blundering snack ban-
   dits, look at each other then back at him.
"in the car?" josh would say.
"—in the garage," i'd add.
our three giant dogs would tap dance around the creaky wood
   floor in a rollicking mass of shaggy red hair, and either josh or
   me would sheepishly hand someone an oyster cracker.
dad, towering over everybody, would lift only one of his eyebrows
   at all of us. the dogs would stop dancing and eye him warily,
   the whirring fans of their tails shushing down.
 "*sleeping*," we'd whisper.

—

i want the fork of my imagination's heart to be described as jew-
   el-like. all its little tines glinting in the warm lemonlight of
   the seasons cycling their variably stirred wistfulness. and this
   is how i want all of us to dream. and to dream, we must sleep.
   at the end of each day, whatever it is, you have to put it to bed.

if you don't sleep, you can't forget all the things your brain needs to scrub clean. imagine hanging on to all the things? no.

it can't always be your turn. you have to climb down off the lookout.

you have to let them go quiet.

you have to let them go.

—

reading is a way of pre-dreaming, of setting a stage. it's the last thing i do in bed every night, the thing that sings me to sleep.

"a metaphor of limitlessness is created by the very real limit of an actual umbrella indoors," sarah says. she says that we want to feel both wet and dry. she says this while looking out at the audience (me) from under a real umbrella beneath a fiction of rain. her eyes (also, i suppose, fictional) are imaginary-puddle-blue.

"i don't suffer from silence," says marcel on the next page, as if answering a question nobody asked. "i could be two days without speaking. i wouldn't suffer at all." the theater's ceiling is pretending to rain on him about this.

i could be two days. i could be eight days. i could be eight hundred days. instead, i'm just one. and i'm putting it to bed. did you know that one day on venus is longer than one year on venus? it's how something turns and the whims of its orbit that determines this. marcel frowns at me.

"two days," he repeats, then speaks only in mum, the language of fish.

"no matter what we do," i assure him, "real things will never out-
number imaginary things."

sarah nods, pleased that we all understand this. i yawn.

her umbrella has a picture of the sky inside.

wing

i guess R is for rick. and rick. and the other rick. disappointment, discomfort, and an accident. where did i get on this memory train of men? i'd like to get off, please. as in to depart, to deplane, to exit, escape. climb down the ladder to the edge of the track where the car slows down enough so i can take the beautiful ballerina-leap i want to wing over the wildflowers that pepper the line, land as deft as a dragonfly, small silent helicopter of summers, foregone sparks flying and me flying off, undetected. straight over the boundary of remembering ricks where i can hit the grass barefoot running and let the train duck into a mountain pass all dark and fast and jangly, come out the far side of the tunnel's deep shadow without me, keep going.

volumes

1 "if one leaves things alone they get less clear by themselves,"
you said. i was watching lonely things turn circles in the snow.
a winter-bird with one bad foot. the owls keep swooping down
from the rafters and stealing bits of yarn from our hats. the weight
of intimation heavy and cold on our shoulders.

2 i can't do this quietly, our hodge-podge piles that don't get
divided, the crumbled chapters of the test, soft flaky flesh-toned
erasers of our bodies worn down to smudging. i needed a good
pair of winter glasses to slide down my nose, to wipe your eyes
clean, to cancel us out.

3 "we should be arranged on the road and treated as outlaws of
probability," you said. i am trying to step out of my shoes, and
they keep filling up with snowflakes. your insistence to frostbite
my feet. past-tense of you to follow me around like a glittery
ghost, kicking my snowdrifts, my toppling promise of forfeit.
you wear your history like a fur hat. but what does your hair look
like in the morning? or in the layered mirror of an icy puddle, the
wind whistling your dissonant ear?

4 the lines are so long. you string me up on the clothesline with
bits of torn underwear and crooked clothespins. you arrange
me in the yard with the pine cones, looking for clues. a cat on
the banister. an abandoned granite bird-bath. a half-eaten apple
hanging frozen, candied on the branch. i forget how to fill up the
spaces between things.

5 the borders of our desires melt and reconstruct us and move through time like foreign countries. two women wash up and you implicate my shady arrangements of weather. the weight of missing words sinking your footprints in front of me. the graceful precarious fault-lines of our tongues and fingers, jagged jelly-jar crack through the bottom of our shifty alliance.

6 strung along with all the wrong words. "our lacking sentences," you said, "would be terrifying with vagueness- if we stopped making pictures." i am one woman, two lips, two big pupils that you keep in your chest like charms against kidney stones or a day without birds. like our waterlogged use of the word "home", how i keep uncrumpling it, to float it like a paper boat in the corners of your eyes.

7 "i thought you wanted to contain everything," you said. the clamoring noises of the morning that slip dreams from our fingers like sand. the container doesn't fit. i tiptoe the edges, faulted, silent.

8 the special debacle of language plays us like a word puzzle. a book-full. like hopscotch, scratched into wet cement, breaking the rules with the board, the soft things that crust up to accidental permanence; my mistakes are like this. my skirting between the lines, the compulsive script that runs down the length of my body, proving my inadequacy as an actress, mapping me backwards like tracks in the snow.

9 you press your lips, looking away. take one breath at me with pursed eyes, as if headed underwater for the final time. "as if this search for a pace were useful," you said, "like sanding the handrail or wearing raincoats." our conversations are swallowed by the same dusty stories, told over again and again, every other page torn out, graying in the gutter with the bean-pods and pigeon bones.

10 you were mocking me from the back of a mirror. the silver glimmer of multiplication. wind picks up from the sea, songbirds stutter and grow cold. it's never been our fault: a mouth has meaning built into it.

RED WONDER is the wonder of accidents, the endless pointed what-ifs, false alarms, real alarms. it's the wonder of all-of-a-sudden and of fallen cherries smashed on the bottom of your gray shoes, and of having sidewalk-slipped across them like marbles, their spent blossoms decorating the fringe of median like an impending scandal, like ruffles. red wonder is for the moment when you realize someone shouting from the top of the parking garage has started to sing instead, for the cardinal couple hopping together under the feeder tossing each other seeds, their crimson feathers bright as fruit against the drape of muffling snow. red is licking the sweet strawberry candy and smearing it like lipstick over your mouth, for making kissy-faces at yourself in the mirror, is the mystery of a secret note passed from fluttering hand to hand under the desks, of secret admirers and the blush of being watched from some other part of the room, the knowing that someone has fallen in love with the way your cheekbone lifts and tilts in the overhead light when you have a question you aren't asking. red wonder is the wonder of open heart surgery and what that means, of the deliciously traversable line between your crush and his skin, of a tiny fire truck zooming this way and that way along the carpet, silent but for the animating magic of some little someone's invisible breath.

birds

i didn't mean to say it that way. sometimes i open my mouth and a bird pops out, all flap and feather and. sometimes Someone goes to give me a hug and finds my back is filled with birds. "i'm sorry," i'll say, not meaning it. the tighter he tries to hold me, the fussier the birds get. when one starts pecking at his hand, even the teensiest goldfinch, he releases me and backs away, incredulous.

"wait—can those *fly*?" he says without saying it.

i shrug, which makes the feathers cross together like scissors or prayers. "it's just all these tiny wings," i say.

every time i miss something or someone, i grow a new bird. they blossom from my back like stop-motion cherry blossoms, or like bougainvillea, you know all that giant thorn and romantic draping. in san francisco, people drove under curtains of crimson bougainvillea to get into their garages. not many people had garages so only a few people. i imagined they must all be filled with flowers, the garage-haver having to step gingerly out of the car to avoid crushing tissue-paper rock roses, delicate pearly jasmine, spiky rosemary and dancy rhododendrons and trumpet lilies and hushes of emerald ivy quietly creeping everywhere.

outside, the sidewalk settles into its grit. the fog washes in from the coast, wordlessly smudging everything in its ocean mist. i miss that place beautifully, terribly. i wish i were there now.
a red-tailed hawk blooms on my back, its curved ochre talons at the ready.
Someone turns around and runs so fast they lift right off the ground.

dear mister,

when you read this, a blank page with a single dark frame, all my little words that are invisible inside.

when you read this, imagine the evening, hocus-pocus, pick up a book and set it down again, follow me when i pull on my coat to tramp out into the snow, the moon like a thin slice of cake, imagine my hands through my mittens, all language hushed, stars in a sugar chrysalis spilled over the inner lip of the mind.

when you read this, think how one condition is never sufficient for another. how to boil oneself in love, poise, dip a spoon to cool it. stand under the sky, hands in surrender, hear the mocking of the tall trees down the street, and you'll see hundreds of black birds, or perhaps thousands of people, walking through the sky to an unknown shrine behind the familiar black horizon.

when you read this, think of your happiness, but desperately want one of those summer storms that bends trees into strange shapes, makes the leaves rattle on their slender stems, littling the world, making everything precious or new, and even as you sleep on the side where you do not sleep, watch the birds out the window, stay up all night and try to find out. half-dreaming, half-lying, half-floating, half-poem, be the good part, the true part, be true enough.

triangulation

the language of lanterns is exquisitely dumbfounded. is the imag-
ination in the head? like how if someone wants me i'm outside
the house of myself hiding, dropping ice chips in the flowerbed
and snapping the heads off the daisies to tuck them under my
tongue. *can i come in? i can't hear you*, he'll say, and i'll be grin-
ning hilariously not because i'm glad but because i'm nervous
and i can't help it and because i'm trying to answer but my mouth
is filled with yolky yellow and petals. *this is why nobody can un-
derstand you*, he says, knocking on the wall, shaking his head, at
which point my own head will garden my heart straight out of
my body and wrap the windows with climbing vines so neither
of us can see inside.

just at the edge, where solid and liquid mix to make mud

i was probably eight years old, but does this have to be about me? i ate a frog-egg. and i mean i really ate it. i didn't just lick it or put it on my tongue and spit it out, i actually ate it. i was in a pond. i was covered in muck. it was so lord-of-the-flies or something. i didn't have a lilypad in my eye. the ground didn't crack open like a speckled brown egg with a yellow yolky duckling inside. instead, it was slimy and slippery and slipped down my throat and nothing happened. jolie rolph was sitting next to me in the pond, lakeblue eyes big like globes, wet with reflected pondwater. swimming minnows. something. i think we were naked. i think we were tired of kissing captured (terrified, peeing) frogs and toads and were going for something more consequential. we were waiting for some magic to happen. to rise up from out of the muck and prove itself, like it does. does it?

there was a church on that island. bear island, it was called. in the summertime we paddled a canoe across the lake to the island. once we brought a whole garbage bag full of barbie and her friends and their endless pink and white artillery. it sat on the bottom of the canoe all the way to the island. sloshy. i don't think we ever even played with it. there was always a more interesting Very Important mission to take on. like that church, for example. there was something spooked about it, something always-autumn, something like a bucket to catch a leak that has a long way to fall. that hollow plunk or thump. jolie rolph and i would take these Very Important pilgrimages to the church, which was on

some other edge of the island, just to spook ourselves. the titilla-
tion of some old-fangled danger. shades of brown. stain-colored,
iodine. abandoned birds' nests. colonial ghosts. witch-dust. in
the winter when we couldn't canoe we cross-country skied across
the lake. all winter long, back and forth. walking on water.

in my memory of that island, there's something very salem
witch-trialy about it. something tutuba, scarlet letter, something
rustling the autumn underbrush. some kind of trap we never
got caught in, but that danger was so delicately infused into ev-
erything. sun through birches, sun sinking into water, long af-
ternoon lakeshadows shaped like mysterious creatures, like in-
trigue, dangerous ideas. all of it you could walk right through,
the light and dark moving, falling across your eyes in ancient
patterns like water seems to. we were a maple-people. a lake-peo-
ple. a canoe-people with some sunwarmed water splashing the
bottom around our sneakers. it's how lorine says *fish / fowl / flood
/ water lily mud / my life*, that makes me love her.

:

what's a giant bird that starts with a vowel? it's not a riddle. the
church was in the forest, and so was the frogpond because every-
thing on the island was. it was a cut-out chunk of new england
forest floating belly-side-up and all by itself in the middle of that
giant lake. is there a shadow under an island? i was never really
afraid of the dark, but i was afraid of the shadow of our little
sailboat. treading water in my smudgy tangerine life-jacket, i'd
imagine that the shadow was a whale and it was looming just un-

der my feet, waiting for it's chance to gobble me. the lake-whale became an almost mythological creature, showing up every time i swam from the boat. i never told anybody. nobody knows about the lake-whale but you and me.

so but that bird- that bird lived in the forest with everything else, on the way to the church. it's nest was high up in this tree. was it birch? maple? something. a lot of birch out there. skinny white trunks you could bend like licorice. dug-up bone-colored. the nest was enormous. at the edge of my mind, it's as big as a tree-house. five stories high in its licorice branches. if the nest was that big, jolie rolph reasoned, how big was the bird? it wasn't *egret* or *osprey*, definitely not *ostrich*- that bird could fly. i never saw it. i imagined its wingspan as big as a rooftop. a bird who could drape itself over a crumbling church. a bird who casts a shadow big as a boat. i recently discovered the largest flying bird who ever lived. its name was (is) *Argentavis Magnificens*, which means "magnificent argentine bird". six-million years ago, Magnificens wandered the andes mountains and the treeless plains of argentina with a wingspan of 19 to 26 feet, a height of 6.5 feet, and a weight of 140 to 180 pounds. feather-size for this bird is estimated to have been about 5 feet long. though it may have needed a downhill running-start into a headwind to get off the ground, it is said that Magnificens was an excellent glider, like a sail plane.

how much do you think a five-foot-long feather would weigh?

spring

at the tip of the day i remember what's wrong with my self-centered self. there's a deep mirrored bed under my bed where the bud nosed up.

maybe i need to try harder.
 G says maybe you're trying hard enough.
 a man parks in a perfect parallel and floats out of the car.
 everyone's pausing on the just-flowered path today. petal, petal, leaf.
 we make a moving garden.

the night was electric blue, which says everything about everybody this morning. rainbow of feet drift by, green bird hovers, another rainbow of feet. a bookmobile looks like a bird, then ice cream truck, pickup filled with flowers, sunshine school bus, toy train, red joyride, unicycle, blue trike, glorious clamor, light, rainbow, bird, clamor, light.

a man is flinging his lavender hat to a swoop of pigeons. he is closing his eyes above the downward shrug of his jacket, his face exposed to the sky.

shine

everything

"wait," greg says when he sees the medical center card on the fridge, "his name is Nickel Noe?" it's tacked there via the mysterious attraction between a colorful octopus-drinking-a-cup-of-coffee magnet and my new refrigerator. "wow, that's a weird name. i like it."

these are weird times, i think. i actually own that refrigerator? i own a refrigerator? we're still in our sock-feet and pajamas and suddenly i feel like holding hands.

"i think he's german," i say. "maybe french? he does the thing where you say one sound like another."

greg turns away from the card and smiles at me. his face is soft and bright. *everything is going to be okay,* the smile says. it always says that.

"what if it isn't?"

"what?" he says, collapsing a little at the corners. "what if what isn't?"

"everything," i say.

the beginning

"your wision," he says. "how is your wision?"

"my what?"

"your wision."

QUICK, his pen says, posing, poised, possibly annoyed to be pausing. he is writing down everything i say. *he is my strange new stenographer,* i think. stenographer of my body. topographer? these enemy camps. sunken ships. how long have they been there? nobody knows. he is my oceanographer.

"your *WISION*," he repeats, as if my ears might not be working. his eyes are dark and watching, his face is face-colored, long, unfamiliar. he wears a sharp collar, midnight tie and a lab coat. it's noon. the coat is starched white as a wall. i imagine his family back home, whatever home is, how proud they must be, his academic office, fancy desk, the professor, neurologist, scientist, all the right (wrong) questions shimmering under the surface of his inky eyes like plankton. or maybe he's the black sheep, the oddball, maybe he was supposed to be an artist or a plumber or a priest, draped or drenched or singing, a color-wheel. or maybe he's an orphan. bravely sailing the deeps of other families' brain scans, a wheel of trembling strangers forever in his waiting room, wringing its hands.

"your *vision*, Sis," my dad says in a low voice beside me. "he's asking about your *vision*."

"oh, my vision," i say. the plankton drift nimbly in all directions, easily escaping my big, dumb whale. "my vision is fine."

physiology picnic

> my brain attaches to stories. i read about it. all the various lobes seem to be involved. i look at the article's illustration of my brain, which looks like everyone's brain (or so these kinds of illustrations seem to imply) but i happen to know now that mine has patches, little sequins of light where some of it has worn away. i spend time wondering if maybe the whole thing is made of light,

actually, underneath, like a star with a sea cave around it. where the cave wears away in high tide, those little patches, and then you can see through with all the luminous fishes. remember how leonard cohen said it? *there's a crack in everything—that's how the light gets through.* i wonder. greg's favorite old corduroy pants have bare spots like this, where you can't see the velvety stripes anymore—i wonder if it's something like that. there are shooting stars in my brain, i think. *ping!* i remember something about the corpus coliseum, that it's like a muscled bridge that connects one side to the other. maybe brain sides are like parallel universes...i like this idea—*ping!*—so i write it down. i sometimes think (with one or both sides) of the whole thing as a galaxy. like the milky way. because it shines like that.

i climbed into a giant magnet so they could take pictures of it, kind of like how we send satellites into space and take pictures of the earth from that galactic perspective. everything is backwards, though: instead of going way outside, the magnet knows how to go way inside. a light-miner. *this is how gems are dug up*, i think, sitting in the waiting area, amber-bright autumn sun draping its way in through the tall windows full of an evergreen hedge and the

shimmery/hard morning street beyond
it. imagine a little miner, drawn as if
magnetically, finding a subterranean
roomful of herkimer diamonds, ici-
cle-white, or amethyst points, sparkling
like a bed of glass irises from the walls,
bellflower, anemone, all glittering eerily
like planets in a secret dark, reflecting
the stage-managed light of the miner's
humble headlamp. imagine they were
there all along! right under our feet?
the earth is made of crystals and mud
and flowers. they fill up my heart and
chase everything around in there for a
while, in the soft identical upholstered
wooden chairs, one of which i am sit-
ting on the edge of. in my cool jittery
heart where a rabble of tiny terrified
baby bunnies seem to be hopping in all
directions, looking for something warm
and familiar, looking for deliverance
from an undefined trap.

i had to take my nose ring out
in the little locker room closet.
"don't let me forget it!" i said,
carefully bending the little wire
hoop askew so i could slip it
off. "i won't," greg said, and

took up the whole doorway like a raised drawbridge when he said it. it was the first thing i did when i got to college. the man who pierced it was covered head to toe in tattoos, a million shining little hoops lining his boot-colored earlobes all the way up in a silver fringe; it was a small second story smudged-window parlor of an old colonial building in a hip little cityful of them, a colorful speckle on the tiny coastline of new hampshire. i think it was raining. it was probably late september. the room smelled like rain and the orange *Dial* antibacterial liquid soap that he told me to rinse it with for two weeks after he'd plunged the long needle through my nostril, shown me my own needled face in a little plastic hand mirror, and slipped into the hole a single shining hoop: mine. i still love the smell of that soap, antiseptic and musical like controlled reckless-

ness, pained pleasure, shiny
new self-government, wonder.

into the magnet i brought nothing but
my nakedness under soft cotton cloth-
ing. no buckles or snaps allowed, noth-
ing shiny. no adornments or autonomy,
even though i climbed in alone— just
me and the magnet. greg sat in a chair
off to the side (i could kind of see him
out of the corner of my eye) and proba-
bly had on those old corduroys and we
both were wearing squishy rubber ear-
plugs the nurse gave us. i thought he'd
like the weird sounds we'd heard the
magnet makes. mostly it sounded like a
siren, a tsunami warning, a monstrous
industrial alarm clock. *wake up! wake
up! wake up!* i tried to harmonize with
the tones so i could make friends with it
because i was naked under my clothes
and it had me surrounded, but it was
mostly like offering a handful of ber-
ries to a thousand-pound bear, know-
ing you're alone in the woods with him
and that's all you have. mostly i brought
breathing.

i brought humming and breathing and complete stillness. mostly i brought humming, breathing, complete stillness, and my imagination. i had to. and where can i ever go without it anyway? i didn't imagine the sequins in my corpus coliseum just yet, the smudges of starlight that were shining inside the cage of my skull, because i didn't know they were there. but the magnet found them: i'd brought them with me.

beauty

there are so many things that can go wrong with the head. then again, it's astonishing what the head does on its own, how many things are going right *all the time* in there in order for us to function. whoever you are, you should have your head examined.

the first time i saw the inside of my head, i was astonished. it almost didn't even matter that there were weird little planets of light polka-dotting it like some disorganized constellation, and at first—utterly unlike myself—i didn't even wonder what the constellation was picturing (a crystal tree? a hunter's bell? a starfish of misshapen, huddled birds?), because it was so beautiful and strange.

i pointed, lightning-fingered. "that's my *brain*?"

"yes," dr. Noe said, both his eyes and mouth smiling warmly. "this is your brain."

i cocked my head this way and that way, bewildered, beholding. *my brain.*

"you see here," he said, growing serious. he waved his fingertips over the constellation. "the brain, it has been attacked." i know, i know, i thought, but there it *is!* all of it felt so sci-fi. greg, sitting beside me, was leaning forward in his chair, looking dazzled himself, which is not a common look for him (he does not usually lean forward in his chair). his dazzle was contained though, his face still serious and relaxed, his surprise cloistered in the eyes and in the leaning. this is a major difference between us. the capacity to contain a dazzle. judging by the look i was getting from dr. Noe, i imagine my face (the outermost expression of my head and its galaxies), as usual, betrayed me.

i think he keeps talking and greg keeps listening.

i don't take my eyes off the brain.

"scientists are buffoons," i sigh. "not because they're rational, but because the cosmos is *irrational*."
greg looks at me like suddenly a sunflower has sprouted out of my ear.

dr. Noe stops and smiles this knowing smile, which spreads across his face like a rainbow, beaming at me like a lightsaber.
"she's fast enough for you, old man," i say.

i don't take my eyes off the brain.

"the stars are sighing through their scaffolding," i say, "on which beads of wonder build but do not drip."

greg closes his eyes and seems to fall down into a very deep well of something. i can feel the emptiness of the bucket on its way down, the cracks and fissures along its outer edge.

dr. Noe looks out the window longingly, and all the trees let go their leaves in a sudden september gust, a wild ochre flourish and swirl.

i don't take my eyes off the brain.

"are we still trying to electrocute flies?" i demand. "do you know if a fly is an electrical conductor?"

greg reaches out and zaps my arm with the cling peach tip of his index finger, then holds my hand resolvedly like we're about to jump off of something together.
dr. Noe spins the computer screen away from me and begins typing furiously, which makes all the star-spots rearrange into the shape (which i can't see) of a butterfly startling up from its flower.

i don't take my eyes off the brain.

everyone's been asking me all these questions, about The Episode, about what my face did. since i'm not totally sure who i am or who i love or how i arrived, not exactly ("good writing is about telling the TRUTH!"), i challenge the doctor to a duel.

greg, who opposes the idea of dueling, stares straight ahead as if pretending he doesn't know me. *maybe he doesn't!* i think, getting hysterical.

"everybody can relax," says the doctor, who seems to know all of the answers to everything and none of the answers to everything at the same time. he straightens the row of pens in his breast pocket importantly, which look like shark teeth.

"i'll duel," says the shark, in a very throaty/raspy (classic) shark voice. the words sound garbled, as if from a mouth with too many teeth inside. as if from a million miles underwater. the bottom, maybe, where only the blind ones circle, their bellies brushing the sand like an endless mandala. i remember reading about sand mandalas, and especially that the last thing is the dismantling ceremony. that you can put the sand on your altar and /or sprinkle it on the head of someone who is dying. is my brain dying?

"is my brain dying?" i say.

greg shifts uncomfortably in his chair.

dr. Noe closes his eyes and lifts his chin skyward, as if in prayer.

"yes," he says. "and no."

"that's a non-answer," i point out.

when he opens them a tiny crab scuttles by. its legs make cartoon crab-scuttling sounds, like it's wearing tap-shoes. click/clack.

"it's maybe, how to say this," he murmurs, narrowing the eyes at me, "too alive."

i don't take my eyes off the brain, and the room goes quiet around me for a long moment. greg and dr. Noe are talking but i don't really hear them. the leaves outside make a little ruffle of sound around what feels like floating. i want to clear my throat, but cannot. *what are all those spots?* i want to ask. *what do they mean?*

and most importantly: are they so, so strange and beautiful? or is it me who is strange—and they're not beautiful at all?

drop

he poked a hole in my back and now my spine is trying to stitch itself back together again.

i saw my spinal fluid. he held it up to the light.

"very clear," he said.
"hi, mom," i said. i couldn't see her from where i was laying but could feel her cringe.
"hi, sweetheart," she squeaked.

i imagined it glittering like the fluid inside a snowglobe, a little bird or house or flower growing inside. when he shook the vial, it played music. a tinkling, plinking tune, tiny, that everyone both recognizes and can't remember, but associates with starry things and times. this is the stuff that keeps me upright, and quiet, that lubricates my body's journey through all the mundane and whimsical windows of living.

"it looked like water," she said afterward, shell-shocked.

"it did," i agreed, keeping as much to myself as i could under the circumstances.

–

i wake up late and dizzy. i don't tell about it, except a couple quietly-times when nobody hears me and i don't really want them to anyway. "i'm dizzy," i say to the coffeepot, as if testing it out to see what happens when i push it off the ledge of my mouth. my dad has already been out and has returned with bottles of painkillers. the name brand bottles are colorful and confident, lined up on the kitchen table like circus performers. i always buy the generic ones, they're cheaper. the bottles are white and plain and they wait plainly in the hush of the cupboard, indifferent, their yawns catching on. my mom bustles back and forth making toast, for which i am not hungry. everything on the kitchen counter wobbles and waves mildly when i turn my head, like we're all underwater, but i don't want anything else to be removed or examined so i say nothing at all.

—

picture me: curled on my side like a baby animal, my sky-blue gown open in the back, spine exposed, zigzagging in peachy divots, all its little hills and valleys naked and lit up on the table. i don't know what to do with my hands. the nurse is in jeans and a hot pink sweater (why is she wearing jeans?) and she holds me with slight pressure, bracing me at the hip and the shoulder for the impending puncture.

"a little prick," she says. "deep breath."

i breathe in a whoosh, like an ocean my breath inflates me, is a little inflatable life boat that i follow as i am stung by a strange, silent bee.

that's just the first thing.

when the big sting comes it's not a stinger at all, but a needle.

i feel something vital and secret and precious leaking, like light being siphoned.

"now it comes, drop by drop," he says quietly. i like his rich accent, the music the edges of the words play. i am being drained like a swimming pool. it hurts. i breathe as slowly as my lungs will allow. i am a hot air balloon sailing on my breath. i cut through clouds, diaphanous, a shred of a dream of a bird.

"try to relax," the nurse says. "relax."

i soften my wings and plummet, then right myself again, afraid. my body doesn't want to give this up.

dream

my dreams have been getting progressively weirder.

last night, for example, there were hundreds of goats who lived on a ski mountain. it was springtime, green and true. the goats, when they died, just collapsed in piles, strung around the grassy slopes like jewelry. the other goats ran in small herds, faster than anything, and when they ran over the piles of bodies, the bones turned to dust and evaporated. this was how they completed the cycle.

see what i mean? what the hell kind of dream is that?

mine

everything in the woods is getting wavy. i don't know how else exactly to say this.

"like you're off-balance?" greg says, watching my face with his waterlily eyes.

"no," i say. "like everything is moving but when i pause to catch it in the act, it stops."

a little frog of worry leaps off and lands in the pond with a tiny splash. he kisses my head, wordless, but i can hear the ripples.

when i'm walking alone with the dog, i stop every few steps on the flat part of the trail to test it. i land on one foot and look around, my other foot dangling in space behind me, or in front, or on the side. sometimes i hop around, test myself turning. perfect landing, i stick it every time like a wilderness gymnast. in the wilderness of the wooded park by my house, i test my body to test my brain. with the trees, the puddles, the million yellow leaves having fallen. the leaves in their rustling applaud my grace, my perfect stops, my starts and leaps and ability to balance even when the whole world is waving at me.

they tested my brain with a giant magnet in a cold, metal room and my brain failed the test.

because my burglar heart and i stole it, and leapt out with it backwards. because we fall through space with it, hollering, drop stars as we go plummeting by.

because it all might be backwards—imagine!—because of what i brought with me.

because it played that song when they shook it.

because it shines like that.

visitation

you will move far away from home.

you will fall in love easily and repeatedly and with everything and everything will break your heart. the lamp of your heart will break every day. the same things that light it up will break it. you will keep plugging it back in and it will keep lighting up and breaking, lighting up and breaking. the best you'll be able to figure is that it fills and grows new circuits and reassembles itself while you are sleeping. every night you will open your heart back up and dream your dreams so you can fall in love more tomorrow. every night, you will survive.

you will first fall in love with two dogs who love you back but will not be yours. then you will get your very own dog, and you will name her Olive, because that is the most beautiful name. she will imprint on you because she will be much too young when she needs you to rescue her, like a teeny golden bear you can hold in your hand, and soon she will become a golden coyote in a red bandana but for her whole life you will call her your duckling because she will follow you everywhere, wait for you anywhere, and do anything for you. you will trek across the country as a pair, a living duet. this will be the first time of many. she will have an accidental litter of puppies on the other side in the leaky carport of a muggy southern suburb during a flood, and you will sleep outside with them for weeks in solidarity with her. when they are old enough, you will give them away from a box at the health food store. one puppy will be jet black with bright blue eyes. she will go home with a gentle, kind-handed man with dark skin whose eyes shine and match hers. Olive will be relieved that it's just the two of you again. you will sing that song to her, "just the two of us, we can make it if we try, just the two of us, you and i." it is her favorite song. you will sing it again and again. you will leave that soggy town together and anywhere you are together from now on you will be home. you will survive.

when you go home for the holidays, your grandma will be forgetting everything. "who owns all these trees?" she will say when you go pick her up in your mom's car. she will have her overnight bag and her cream puffs and christmas pajamas and you will be driving back along the pine-rimmed ribbon of the rural highway and it might be snowing, just some lazy festive flakes floating down like tired confetti. "who owns this land?"

men will frighten you. men will dismiss you. men will look you in the eye and lie to you. they will say horrible things to you and will kiss you disgustingly without asking. men will do many things without asking. they will ignore you and talk down to and over you. men will take things that are not theirs, bodies and babies and credit and countries. men will look everywhere but in your eyes. while you're on your back in their bed, men will surprise you by pretending to strangle you. men will disarm you. men will puff up their bodies and loom over yours menacingly.

men will call you disturbing names that will ring in your head for years. even when they brought you as their date, instead of kissing you on new year's eve they will kiss another woman right next to you. on your walk home, alone, you will hear hooting and fireworks in the distance. you will find a fake potted palm tree on the street. you will carry it upstairs and put it in the window. the following year one of your roommates will decorate it with tinsel and colored lights.

men will listen to and want to hear you. they will hold your hand while you're crossing the street and in airplanes and cars and they will pull over at the strawberry patch because they'll remember how you love strawberries. men will sing to you and soothe and settle you and surprise you with tulips. when you don't have a pocket, they will let you keep your chapstick in theirs. men will call you Special and Brilliant and Magical and call themselves Fae or Fools. men will give you their lucky bead and you will put it in your hair. men will watch you laughing across the room and fall in love with you on the spot. men will play with your dog and put a blanket on her when it's cold. they will offer to carry things for you. not just your many heavy boxes of books but also other, interdimensionally heavy things. they will read your writing and let it fizz their own heart open, feel its lurch and swoop and swirl. and when you want them to, they will touch your body exactly how you like and will sail you straight out of the room, to the moon. you will survive.

you will live in a grand toppling city, right in the bright beating heart of it. there will be parades for no reason, and monks who live in a big orange house on the corner with their colorful prayer flags and swishing brown robes and singing bowls. you will have a cherry-red bike and will ride it all over. Olive will learn to play basketball in the park and a game she makes up with giant eucalyptus bark strips in the courtyard behind the cathedral up the block with the stone saint in the fog on top. you will fall in love with many giant cypress trees that all reach together away from the ocean. all your friends will be artists and writers. you will work at a coffeeshop, riding your bike across the park to get there so early it's still dark out, and you will fall in love again, this time with both the writers and a ragtag gang of morning-merry baristas. one in particular is a problem because he will be magical and he will be married. he will be christian and peruvian and musical and bird-like in the way he will flit around you, smiling, avoiding your eyes. you will have dreams that he remembers and he will have dreams that you do. he will lead you on for a long time but will never leave his wife or his god for you. you will fall apart so completely that you will miss your first grandfather's funeral, choosing instead to stay in the city with Olive and climb to the tops of hills and cry. your brother will hold a grudge and then let the grudge go. a few years later the bird-man will crack your heart in half and eat his half in the dream. not right away, but eventually. you will eventually understand that it was a dream heart, dream of a bird-heart. this is how you will learn how to write. by falling in love with everything and understanding it. you will write your heart out and you will learn and survive.

you will live in a van. you will live in a cave. you will live in a tent, on the road, on the beach, on the fly. you will live in a window, paycheck to paycheck, or without a paycheck by the seat of your pants. you will live vividly, every day like the first and the last and every day in between. in between days, you will continue to dream. you will learn to dream better. in one dream you will sit in a sunny small kitchen while your grandpa is cooking and singing and you will say something that makes him throw his head back laughing and you will wake up in your own bed laughing along. you will survive.

at one point there will be the accidental kernel of a child you will not have. you will have to wait with the kernel in your belly one whole month for the appointment and you will feel like a pirate walking the plank. despite your decision or maybe because of it, you will name the kernel Grace. many years will go by and though sometimes you will count them on your fingers, how many she would be, you will never regret it. you will count other things, too, pages and stars and plants and petals and spring geese in their honking clamorous V in the sky. you will go along just fine with that little ghost sharing your body. she will swim. you will survive.

you will fly to new york when your first grandma dies, and your dad will weep while telling a story and your uncle joe will cross himself and toss an acorn into her grave. with you sitting on her bed at the hotel your mother will tell you the story of when she was sixteen and her father died in the bathroom while she was on the phone with her friend after school and no one else was home and she didn't know. she will tell about how your grandma screamed at her and how the neighbor men broke down the bathroom door and how she saw them carry him out of the house in a body bag. it will be devastating and horrifyingly crystalline and all at once you will understand everything about your mother, will understand it from that point on. you will get up very early to fly to florida when your favorite aunt who was your second grandma dies, and you will be so upset at 5am you will take some pills someone gave you on an empty stomach and will have to ask the airport shuttle guy to pull over on your way out of the city in the dark so you can throw up in the gutter. within months your second grandpa will start getting mixed up, losing things, becoming increasingly disoriented and confused and anxiously clutching the tiny dog who liked to nap in your second grandma's lap. he was young and proud once and walked your mother down the aisle. your mother will be vigilant, will stop sleeping. he will be diagnosed with Alzheimer's. later, on the radio, you will hear a doctor say dementia is forgetting where you put the fork, and Alzheimer's is forgetting what the fork is for. your second grandpa will have to be moved from the long-shining paradise of his home to the locked-down memory ward of a nursing facility nearby and the anguished, lost look on his proud face when you visit and pace the corridors with him will be the saddest thing you will ever see in your whole life. he will die before he forgets who you are, which means he will never forget who you are. your grandpa will always remember who you are and you will survive.

at one point in the city you will start getting nosebleeds, but you will not be a casualty of the scene. you will get lost then get a grip and get clean. you will lose your keys. you will lock yourself out. you will only get arrested once and will not get locked up.

you will lock your keys in your car or drop them in a river. one time you will not lock up your red bike when you come home from the coffeeshop to run upstairs for Olive and it will vanish forever. every year you will lose things. every year you will get lighter. you will keep trying to leave yourself places, like a baby on a doorstep. you will not succeed. you will keep opening the door and finding yourself.

there will be a carpenter. a bartender. a drug dealer. a textbook editor. there will be artists, poets, musicians. one will be all three, just like you. because you are both filled with feelings and music and paint he will supernova your heart-lamp with his and blow all your circuits and you will both explode.

there will be a bisexual anarchist and a zen buddhist composer. an alcoholic handyman and a colorblind glassblower. one will be a grade school science teacher. another a quiet hockey player with secret light and long dark eyelashes who smells of ice and reminds you of home. some will talk you up. most will play you down. more than one will play the guitar. you will be growing into a better guitarist than all of them, but none of them will know. there will be a soft-spoken mechanic who will be fourteen years older than you. you will move in together. he will squint thoughtfully into the distance. he will fix your van and kiss your dog and want you to marry him. you will not marry him. you will break his heart magnificently and move away and he will get strung out on drugs and his teeth will fall out and he'll spend his later years in and out of prison. from many miles and states away you will see his yearly mug shots on the internet where he will look increasingly wretched and unhinged. you will be sorry you saw them but every year you will look again. you will feel the deep small shatter of shame and disgrace every time but remorse won't unravel you. you are growing and you made the right choice. you will survive.

you will meet a teacher who will change your life because she will polish the light of your eye and how you shine it. you will become a writing teacher like her and have hundreds of students. because you are in love with everything you will be a loving teacher and have students who adore you. you will love your community college students the best. they will have names like Logan and Brittany and Colin and Eric and Amanda and Usamah. Usamah will write a story about watching his father and brother get shot and killed in Iraq. his writing will be windswept and bent and beautiful. he will have sad dark eyes like polished garnet and he will always be fully present, his attention glowing at you like a hurricane lamp. Eric will be in recovery and it will be nine in the morning but he will bring everybody candy to share. his spelling will be terrible but his feelings will be breathtaking. he will bring his fat black wagging dog to class and her name will be Casey and she will snore melodiously through the lessons. when someone in the building asks about the dog you will nibble a pink starburst and lie. Colin will be your all-time favorite because come hell or high water with the cards stacked against him he will make his own magic and always have the telltale twinkle of a roving poem in his eye, like it's hopping train cars and scratching hearts in the dirt with a stick. at one point he'll construct a poem for you from your own comments on his poems and you will fold it carefully and keep it forever somewhere so safe and special you can never remember where it is. you will fall in love with all of your students but only run away with them in your heart which they will break and mend and run away with. one day you will write a note to yourself: *they are like kittens. you can't keep them all.* they will save your life many times and have no idea and through the darkest days of your life you will have this, this trying to shine and to teach them, to save you. you will keep breaking and growing and they won't even know. you will survive.

you will meet a man who lives in a northern valley of flowers and birds and rivers and tree-people who wear thick, wooly socks. everything will have a mountain behind it. everybody there will have a dog, there will be as many dogs as people, like a faerie town where everyone has a familiar. the man won't have his own dog, so he will fall quietly in love with yours after he falls in love with you. you will be tuned just right to each other, like radios. when you meet him, you will know totally and right away. you will not fret, you will not weigh or wonder. you will always feel right and safe and yourself around him, always from the very start. this alliance will break your heart too, or he will, you both will. but the breaks won't last and you will fix them carefully together. you are learning. you will teach each other. you will survive. he will be the one who puts the blanket on the dog.

you will get sick. one half of your face will twist painfully over to one side, the whole thing tight and trembling like a bird afraid to fly. you will be anxious and embarrassed and keep putting your face on Olive's face to feel better. you will look like a Picasso painting of yourself. your face will relax and go back to normal, eventually, but there will be a series of strange tests. one doctor will tap your spine, remove its fluid, and see something odd winking there. you will see many pictures of your brain. it will have starry spots all over it. your diagnosis will terrify you and make you think of tidal waves and wheelchairs, but there will be medicine, dripped into your arm every six weeks, and you will continue to walk, run, swim, dance, jump, and twirl as you always have. maybe better. you will be a very good dancer by this time because you have loved music for so long and party people at weddings will enjoy watching you crack other guests up with your dancing while everyone else is just standing around drinking champagne. the doctor says when you are old the stars may make you forget where things are or what they do, forks or words or flint or flowers, but however old you are, you are never as old as you will be. never yet. nevertheless. you will survive.

Olive will get very old and she will die in your arms. her song will play in your heart for the rest of your life. you won't have any idea yet how, how on earth, but somehow—you will survive.

you will always find the flowering fuse and insist on doing things your own way. you will change completely and not change at all. you will often need to see how far things can bend before breaking which means you will bend and bend and then break things. you will write and keep writing and write your first book. having sooner or later learned how to blend more than you break, you will send the book back to visit yourself like a bird with a love note strung to its foot. that is this note and this is that book. you will patch it all back. it will flicker and flare. the rooms of your life will be lit. you will survive.

you will rescue a puppy who looks like a small furry unicorn wearing sunglasses. she will glitter in the sun and it will plug your heart back in. her name will be Pearl. her legs will grow very long. she will learn what makes you laugh and then do it repeatedly. she will like to nudge you with her wet black nose. you will know that Olive sent her and that they both are angels. whenever she comes galloping to find you to tell you something, your heart will break and grow a bright new bloom. you will be in love again. you will be growing. it will all have been true all along: you are here. it goes on. you survive.

thank you

thank you to my beloved writing friends and teachers, each of you both, for your insight, inspiration, and support for me and my work over the years. you hold such a special sparkling place in my inner writing room where my affection for you will always continue blooming no matter how many miles or years apart we are: Truong Tran, Toni Mirosevich, Britta Austin, Diana Aehegma, L.J. Moore, Rick D'Elia, and the rest of our bright-eyed and mischievous san francisco tribe: your presence in my story's arc and my work changed both of them in far too many ways to list here. i'd need another book!

thank you to Peter Krumbach, who notices the best things and shouts them to me across a make-believe hallway filled with our colorful crush of flowers. thank you also to Mike DeCapite, who keeps one eye on the heart and the other on the light so gets it right away.

thank you to my family, whose fellowship is an enchanted harbor, and who have always encouraged me to do and make things with my whole wild imagination and heart.

thank you to my bookseller family at Phoenix Books in Burlington. the reason i'm always late is because i've gotten carried away all morning writing! i treasure your reliable friendship, back-having, and lively company in my reading life, which is my writing life, which is my life.

thank you to Pearly for always being nearby to laugh with and kiss, and for rescuing me from the abyss that was losing Olive. i couldn't have written myself out of that one: you dropped the bright ladder down. you've lifted my spirit with warmth, solace, and joy every day since we met.

thank you forever to Olive, my very dearest of friends, the love of my life. i could never thank you enough. our connection was and always will be everything i really need to understand about the dimensions of the heart, the whole shining thing, which is why this book is for you.

a great, dazzled thanks to the people at Spuyten Duyvil who helped make this collection of shimmerings an actual thing we can hold in our hands. i will remain in humble awe of it always, and of what you all do.

thank you to Heather Woods, delicate word-spinner, gentle mystic, writing-friend-turned-editor, for championing my work. *marmalade* is here in the world because you reached through the twin thickets of time and space to find me twirling about with it like a bunch of butterflies. i will forever thank you for thinking of me and for offering me a garden to put them in.

and thank you, finally, to Greg Davis, whose love is like an open window and a clear pool; who lets me flutter and zoom and who listens on the wavelength, musically, with patience and grace; who discovered me like a lost love letter and swept me into our polyphonic duet where i belong. you are absolutely precious to me: thank you for all of it.

dedications

"notes preceding a new rhapsodic broadcast" is dedicated to Toni Mirosevich

"how to (write a story)" is dedicated to Mike DeCapite

"wishbones" is dedicated to Peter Krumbach

"how to (write a poem)" is dedicated to Truong Tran

"eyes" is dedicated to Greg Davis

"wanderlust home" is dedicated to my mom

inspirations

"in the heart of the heart of the heart of it" is inspired by Etel Adnan's book, *In The Heart of The Heart of Another Country*

"spring" is inspired by work in *The Little Book of Days*, by Nona Caspers

"the thanks-for-the-lift list" is inspired by Thomas Lux's poem, "Ecstasy Notebook"

"stardust" nods to reading Ruth Ozeki's novel, *A Tale for the Time Being*

"letting" is inspired by Tara Roeder's poem, "Picking Up The Pieces"

"red wonder" is inspired by Mary Ruefle's "sadness" poems in *My Private Property*

"on sleep" references Sarah Ruhl's essay, "Umbrellas on Stage", in *100 Essays I Don't Have Time to Write* and Shawn Wen's essay, *A Twenty Minute Silence Followed by Applause*

"flowers" is inspired by reading Abigail Thomas

publishing credits

Thank you to all the journals who've believed in my work over the years and who were the first to publish the following pieces:

A Capella Zoo: "versions"
Eleven Eleven: "it's my birthday" and "when you call"
Flock: "wanderlust home"
Gertrude: "belief systems"
Ghost Proposal: "dear / dear"; "dear, this is a list"; "reasons for reaching"; and "dear, i wanted to tell you something"
Glint: "notes preceding a new rhapsodic broadcast"; "the thanks-for-the-lift list"; "hanging from the sky, swaying with the bee-moons happy (us)"
Hunger Mountain: "spanish for bird"
Panapoly: "stardust"
Postcard Poems & Prose: "vanishing point"
Storm Cellar: "wishbones"
Sugar Mule: "flight patterns" and "just at the edge, where solid and liquid mix to make mud"
The Hunger: "in the heart of the heart of the heart of it"
The Spotlong Review: "shine"
Timber: "winter blues"